BRITISH LIFE
A Century Ago

IMAGES FROM
THE FRANCIS FRITH
COLLECTION

British Life

A Century Ago

TERENCE SACKETT

First published in the United Kingdom in 1999 by
Frith Book Company Ltd

Hardback edition 1999
ISBN 1-85937-103-5

Paperback edition 2000
ISBN 1-85937-213-9

Reprinted in February 2001 and June 2001
ISBN 1-85937-213-9

British Library Cataloguing in Publication Data

British Life A Century Ago
Terence Sackett

Frith Book Company Ltd
Frith's Barn, Teffont,
Salisbury, Wiltshire SP3 5QP
Tel: +44 (0) 1722 716 376
Email: info@francisfrith.co.uk
www.francisfrith.co.uk

Designed and assembled by Terence Sackett
Printed and bound in Great Britain by
The Bath Press, Bath

AS WITH ANY HISTORICAL DATABASE THE FRITH ARCHIVE IS CONSTANTLY BEING CORRECTED AND IMPROVED
AND THE PUBLISHERS WOULD WELCOME INFORMATION ON OMISSIONS OR INACCURACIES

Contents

Foreword

ONE of the hazards of working with an archive of the size and scope of the Frith Collection is that you are daily confronted with historical photographs in their thousands. The archive room is congested with them - you flick through drawer upon drawer of exquisite sepia studies of people, streets and buildings, numberless envelopes and boxes of concealed riches waiting to be discovered. It is both treasure house and labyrinth, and the sheer number of photographs can often seem overwhelming.

Yet it is the study of individual images that is so rewarding. It is always important to keep in mind the fact that each picture was taken as a separate exercise by the photographer, and that each depicts real people in a real place at a certain moment in time. It is this extraordinary particularity that differentiates photographs from paintings, and gives them their unique status as historical documents of fundamental importance.

Compiling and writing this book has given me an opportunity to re-acquaint myself with some of my favourite photographs from the archive. Over the past weeks I have taken a modest pile of them aside to write about. Finding out what each has to tell about the past has been both enjoyable and fascinating.

The Frith archive is gradually being transferred onto computer, each image being scanned and stored digitally. It is paradoxical that this most modern technology brings with it an opportunity to take a fresh look at individual images of the past made by an earlier technology. When you view an image on a large screen and zoom slowly in, the experience can be breathtaking. History begins to open itself up to you. You are suddenly able to read shop signs, to study the faces of people staring out at you, to spot the child who has been hiding in a doorway. But zoom in further and the image begins to break up, to fragment into a mess of pixels: even digital technology will only allow you to journey so far. Yet without it, I could not have made the discoveries about the photographs in this book that I did.

I have taken considerable licence with dates. Although the title of this book is 'British Life A Century Ago', I have included images taken up until the 1940s where I felt that there was a continuity of behaviour, such as in farming practices or the working methods of a particular craft.

Finally, I would like to thank all those people who I approached for information about the content of the photographs. Without their enthusiasm and generosity I would not have been able to put this book together.

Francis Frith:
Victorian Pioneer

FRANCIS FRITH, Victorian founder of the world-famous photographic archive, was a devout Quaker and successful Victorian businessman. He was both philosophic by nature and pioneering in outlook.

By 1855 Francis Frith had already established a wholesale grocery business in Liverpool, and sold it for the astonishing sum of £200,000, which is the equivalent today of £15,000,000. Now a multi-millionaire, he was able to indulge his passion for travel. As a child he had pored over travel books written by early explorers, and his fancy and imagination had been stirred by family holidays to the sublime mountain regions of Wales and Scotland. 'What a land of spirit-stirring and enriching scenes and places!' he had written.

Intrigue and Adventure
♦

He was to return to these scenes of grandeur in later years to 'recapture the thousands of vivid and tender memories', but with a different purpose. Now in his thirties, and captivated by the new photography, Frith set out on a series of pioneering journeys to the Nile regions that occupied him from 1856 until 1860.

He took on his travels a wicker carriage that acted as both dark-room and sleeping chamber. These journeys were packed with intrigue and adventure. In his life story, written when he was sixty-three, Frith tells of being held captive by bandits, and of fighting 'an awful midnight battle to the very point of surrender with a deadly pack of hungry, wild dogs'. Sporting flowing Arab costume, Frith arrived at Akaba by camel seventy years before Lawrence, where he encountered 'desert princes and rival sheikhs, blazing with jewel-hilted swords'.

During these extraordinary adventures he was assiduously exploring the desert regions bordering the Nile and patiently recording the antiquities and peoples with his camera. He was the first photographer to venture beyond the sixth cataract. Africa was still the mysterious 'Dark Continent', and Stanley and Livingstone's historic meeting was a decade into the future. The conditions for picture taking confound belief. He laboured for hours in his wicker dark-room in the sweltering heat of the desert, while the volatile chemicals fizzed dangerously in their trays. Often he was forced to work in remote tombs and caves where conditions were cooler. Back in London he exhibited his photographs and was 'rapturously cheered' by members of the Royal Society. His reputation as a photographer was made overnight. An eminent

modern historian has likened their impact on the population of the time to that on our own generation of the first photographs taken on the moon.

Venture of a Life-Time
◆

Characteristically, Francis Frith quickly spotted the opportunity to create a new business as a specialist publisher of photographs. He lived in an era of immense and sometimes violent change. For the poor in the early part of Victoria's reign work was a drudge and the hours long, and people had precious little free time to enjoy themselves. Most had no transport other than a cart or gig at their disposal, and had not travelled far beyond the boundaries of their own town or village. However, by the 1870s, the railways had threaded their way across the country, and Bank Holidays and half-day Saturdays had been made obligatory by Act of Parliament. All of a sudden the ordinary working man and his family were able to enjoy days out and see a little more of the world.

With characteristic business acumen, Francis Frith foresaw that these new tourists would enjoy having souvenirs to commemorate their days out. In 1860 he married Mary Ann Rosling and set out with the intention of photographing every city, town and village in Britain. For the next thirty years he travelled the country by train and by pony and trap, producing photographs of seaside resorts and beauty spots that were bought by millions of Victorians. These prints were painstakingly pasted into family albums and pored over in the dark nights of winter, rekindling precious memories.

The Rise of Frith & Co
◆

Frith's studio was soon supplying retail shops all over the country. In order to gain some understanding of the scale of Frith's business one only has to look at the catalogue issued by Frith & Co in 1886: it runs to some 670 pages, listing not only many thousands of views of the British Isles but also many photographs of most European countries, and China, Japan, the USA and Canada. By 1890 Frith had created the greatest specialist photographic publishing company in the world, with over 2,000 outlets – more than the combined number that Boots and W H Smith have today! The picture on the right shows the *Frith & Co* display board at Ingleton in the Yorkshire Dales. Beautifully constructed with mahogany frame and gilt inserts, it could display up to a dozen local scenes.

Postcard Bonanza
◆

The ever-popular holiday postcard we know today took many years to develop. In 1870 the Post Office issued the first plain cards, with a pre-printed

stamp on one face. In 1894 they allowed other publishers' cards to be sent through the mail with an attached adhesive halfpenny stamp. In 1899, a year after Frith's death, a new card measuring 5.5 x 3.5 inches became the standard format, but it was not until 1902 that the divided back came into being, with address and message on one face and a full-size illustration on the other. *Frith & Co* were in the vanguard of postcard development, and Frith's sons Eustace and Cyril continued their father's monumental task, expanding the number of views offered to shops and the public.

Francis Frith died in 1898 at his villa in Cannes, his great project still growing. The archive he created continued in business for another seventy years. By 1970 it contained over a third of a million pictures of 7,000 cities, towns and villages. The massive photographic record Frith has left to us stands as a living monument to a special and very remarkable man.

Slugs and Cottage Loaves

THE STORY OF DEVON FINE LACE MAKING

MRS FREEMAN works at a floral sprig of Honiton lace outside her cottage door at Honiton in South Devon in 1907 (RIGHT). If the picture had been taken ten years earlier, her customer might have been Queen Victoria herself, whose dressmakers beat a path to Mrs Freeman's Devon door more than once.

Bobbin lace-making has been made in Devon since the 1600s. It is said that the craft was established when Flemish lace-makers fled to England to escape religious persecution. However, there is no evidence for this claim: Honiton had an early history of textile production, and it is more likely that the Devon workers adapted their existing skills to lace when it became a popular fashion accessory. The town itself was a large and important centre for textiles, and over 2,000 workers were employed in the craft by the end of the 18th century.

Honiton lace was made on a pillow stuffed with chopped straw. Hundreds of bobbins and pins might be used to create an intricate lily or cornflower spray. It is said that Devon lace makers, with their roots firmly in fishing and farming, often used fishbones for pins and carved sheep's trotters for bobbins.

Apprentices were taught to watch the lace and not the bobbins, and were scolded it they failed to work up a good speed so that the bobbins glided smoothly over each other - the knack was to twist and not lift them. The amount workers earned for their lace was calculated by spreading it out flat and covering it with shillings. When

Opposite:
Pillow Lace Worker,
Beer, Devon 1901
47861

Below:
Mrs Freeman,
Lace Worker,
Honiton, Devon 1907
58189

they could not see the design any more, they scooped up the coins.

Making lace is said to bring serenity, yet the history of the industry and of the people who worked in it reveals this to be a myth. In fact, the making of Britain's finest laces involved much exploitation and poverty. Most Devon lace-makers were poor, and many of them were fishermen's wives, toiling into the night to make a few extra shillings while their husbands were away on the boats. Many five-year-old orphans attended lace schools, and learned to make simple patterns called slugs and cottage loaves. Soon they, too, were working for an agent twelve hours at a stretch, saving themselves from being 'burthensome to the parish'. Fishermen themselves were not too proud to learn, and supplemented their precarious incomes by turning their hands to the craft when storms prevented the boats from venturing out.

Unscrupulous agents did the rounds of the lace-makers' cottages collecting the sprigs and sprays of floral designs. They sewed them into patterns and sold them for a high price to merchants and smart dressmakers in London. The patterns were incorporated into wedding veils and appliqued on to stoles. The rose was the most common motif, but the sample on the next page includes grapes and vine leaves, which were not characteristic of Honiton designs.

The infamous 'truck system' cut severely into lace makers' incomes: for each shilling earned, half was often paid in the form of food and clothing. In remote districts where agents refused to call, women and girls were obliged to deliver their work. This could take a whole day, and it was often close to midnight before they reached home,

Above:
**Honiton Lace
1913**
65174

Right:
**Lace Worker,
Honiton c1910**
H111501

having trudged miles through dark, lonely lanes.

Lace was so valuable that it was used as a currency. Much foreign lace was smuggled into Britain in the reign of George III. One trader was caught smuggling £90 worth of lace in a turban. To stop the smuggling, excise men halted the carriages of fashionable young ladies in the London parks, slicing the foreign black lace mittens from their hands.

The invention of machine lace almost destroyed hand-made lace in the 19th century. A new lace factory opened in Tiverton, and this soon threatened the very survival of the skills that had been so hard-won. Changing fashions of the time speeded the decline, and the fine hand-made traditional patterns were replaced by poor quality 'rag lace'.

It is unlikely that the Frith picture of Mrs Woodgate (RIGHT) could have been taken if royalty had not intervened. Queen Victoria helped revive the lace industry; among her commissions was the flounce for the Queen's wedding dress, made by a hundred of the finest lace makers in East Devon. Largely thanks to her, Honiton lace was shown at the 1851 Great Exhibition.

Top right:
Mrs Woodgate, Lace Worker, Honiton 1907
58075

Centre:
The Fishing Village of Beer in 1898, Home of Mrs Woodgate
42434

Below:
Honiton Lace 1913
65171

Performing Miracles in Stone

THE SKILLED WORK OF THE CORSHAM CARVERS AND MASONS

Below:
The Masons'
Yard, Corsham,
Wiltshire 1907
57819

OUR CATHEDRALS are miracles of medieval engineering. The men who built them had no hydraulic cranes or hoists to help them. When you see the thousands of tons of stone in the spire at Salisbury, balanced to perfection four hundred feet in the air, it is hard to imagine how the feat was achieved.

Consider the blocks of building stone themselves. They had to be dug out of the ground, squared up, and chiselled into the exact sizes and shapes. Examine the precise joints in the stones of a cathedral spire or arcade and it is clear there was no margin for error. Every part had to fit.

In the photograph (RIGHT), the masons at Corsham in Wiltshire have already worked the miracle: in the yard are the sections of a column that will form part of the arcade of a church. Each of these blocks has been worked from start to finish with a mallet and chisel. First they had to be 'boned'. Then the masons levelled the edges one by one, and gradually punched out the hump left in the centre until the face was totally square and level. Then they turned the stones over, and did the same to each of the other five faces. Then, with the help of templates and callipers, they carved the stones into the individual sections.

At Corsham, masons have been working the local Bath limestones for many centuries. In the industry's heyday there were fifty quarries and five miles of underground tunnels. In the Corsham Yards - including Pickwick's, Lambert's and Copenacre's - the men worked long hours, producing keystones and quoins for houses, churches and buildings all over the country. At the industry's height they could barely keep up with the demand. The finished work was shipped out on the Kennet &

Avon Canal. The Corsham masons passed on their skills to their sons, as they had been doing for centuries. They were a tight-knit community, proud of their craft and conscious of their tradition of fine craftsmanship.

The Frith pictures show the Corsham Worked Stone Co yard in 1907. The quarry from which the stones came was probably close by - there was little point in hauling such colossal stone blocks further than was necessary. In the picture on the opposite page we can see the crane for heavy haulage, and below it a massive hand-saw for cutting the stone into workable blocks. Sawing was a highly-skilled task, and cuts to within a sixteenth of an inch were necessary. After a shallow cut had been made it was the task of the banker masons to finish the forming of the blocks by hand. In the background, under a plain

Above:
The Corsham
Worked Stone Co.
Yard, Corsham,
Wiltshire 1907
57819

good. Specialisation is now the order of the day. Barry Baldwin, who runs part of what was once Lambert's Yard, has now turned his hand to sculpture and casting. There are now only a dozen men left working in the Corsham yards.

Corsham stone is celebrated the world over for its fine grain and quality. The old town buildings, with their steep gables, were formed of local stone, the lines of the streets revealing a unique and pleasing harmony. Many grand buildings in the region are of Corsham stone, including the splendid

Above:
High Street, Corsham, Wiltshire 1904
51471

Below:
Lacock Abbey, Wiltshire 1904
51510

corrugated-iron roof, are the skilled carvers, working at their bankers with hammer and chisel.

In recent years, with the slump in building, times have been hard for the yards. In Corsham many of the smaller yards amalgamated, and these in turn were taken over by larger companies such as the Bath Stone Company. Some yards were forced to shut up shop for

Lacock Abbey, home of the inventor of photography, Fox Talbot. Corsham Court was built in a local variety called Monk's Park stone.

Further afield, Corsham stone can be found in the Royal Exchange and in Capetown, where government buildings incorporate decorative detailing created by masons from this quiet Wiltshire town.

Turned Snakeskin

Serpentine fancy goods from The Lizard peninsula

THE LIZARD is a remote peninsula set at the southern-most point of Cornwall. Its coast is characterised by a chaos of jagged rock ridges fringing the sea. The wild seas that beat the cliffs here have long been feared by sailors. Much of the Lizard's grandeur derives from its unique serpentine rock, which assumes extraordinary shapes and colours. At Kynance the brilliantly-hued rough green stone forms spectacular caves in the cliffs. Their very names conjure up the ancient romance of this mysterious county: the Devil's Letter Box, the Devil's Mouth, the Bellows.

The serpentine stone reveals yet greater wonders when it is polished. The rich colouring it attains has been compared to the sinuous skin of a snake. In the 1850s there was a considerable local industry devoted to turning and forming the stone into a variety of sought-after gift objects. The Penzance Serpentine Works employed twenty craftsmen, and held a stock of 160 tons of rock in their yard. They supplied chess tables, chimney pieces, vases and flower stands, and boasted that 'orders were constantly received from the nobility and gentry at home and abroad'. Prince Albert commissioned decorative serpentine slabs for his Isle of Wight residence at Osborne.

Serpentine souvenirs have been very popular ever since. This photograph is hard to date, but the simple equipment on show - the lathe and various chisels and scrapers - would be the same as were used a century ago. The tall object on the right is probably the first stage of a model lighthouse. These were made in sizes from a few inches to several feet, and were very popular with visitors.

Below:
In a Serpentine Workshop, The Lizard, Cornwall date unknown L62019

Trailing Slip in Waves, Dots and Whorls

LIFE AND TRADITION IN AN OLD WELSH COUNTRY POTTERY

Below:
**Claypits Pottery
at Ewenny, Mid
Glamorgan 1937**
87908

THE PHOTOGRAPH (BELOW) shows Arthur Trevorrow throwing a jug on the wheel at the Claypits family pottery at Ewenny near Bridgend in Wales in 1937.

Beside him are the various examples of his work, beautifully hand-decorated with slip in waves, whorls and dots. On the right, William Jenkins, proprietor, holds an undecorated pot ready for his nephew Tom to decorate.

Such a scene had been commonplace in Ewenny for over three hundred years. At one stage there were a dozen

small family potteries, owing mainly to the substantial deposits of earthenware clay within the parish boundaries.

The first pottery in the area had been established in the 17th century, making it the oldest country pottery in Wales. Throughout the centuries, the Jenkins family and the Morgans, Williamses and others before them, had produced attractive domestic ware for the local people and the Welsh mining communities. The Jenkins' work was always hand-thrown and decorated, and the pottery never became industrialised.

Tom Jenkins, the man wearing the cap in the centre of the picture, was influenced by the great studio potters of the 30s and 40s - craftsman potters of the calibre of Bernard Leach, Michael Cardew and Henry Hammond. He took over the reins of the business from his uncle in 1939. As earthenware gradually went out of fashion, he diversified, and began to throw stoneware, which sold to the growing number of tourists visiting this picturesque part of Wales.

The photograph above shows the Ewenny pottery, sited across the lane, which was owned and run by a different branch of the Jenkins family. The signboard proudly announces that it is the oldest pottery in Wales and has been 'Patronised by Royalty' - Ewenny produced many decorative items for Queen Mary. It carried out commissions for the Ministry of Works in the 1930s, creating a range of garden pots for the many unemployed people who were set to work in horticulture. Some of the round kilns in the background have been dismantled and re-erected at the National Folk Museum at St Fagans.

The Ewenny Pottery near Bridgend is still a thriving concern today, with Alun Jenkins, the present proprietor, and his wife making items of glazed earthenware. They are now the seventh generation of the Jenkins family to run the business, and are a vital part of the living tradition of country potteries in studios all over rural Britain producing fine, individual work.

Above:
The Ewenny
Pottery, Ewenny,
Mid Glamorgan
1936
87669

Spreading the Good News

THE EARLY YEARS OF THE VILLAGE POSTMAN AND THE POSTAL SERVICE

OUTSIDE the Clovelly Post Office (LEFT), postman Roy Fisher accepts the sacks of local post from the Bideford van. Beside him stands the post-donkey, who was vital to efficient and regular deliveries in this isolated village in North Devon.

The view below shows the steep main street of the village, created from flights of steep, cobbled steps. Villagers used donkeys and sleds to carry goods up

Left:
The Clovelly
Postmen, Devon
1936
87551

Right:
The Street,
Clovelly, Devon
1894
33490

Right:
The Postman at
Houghton,
Hampshire 1904
51457

Below:
The Lynmouth
Postman,
Countisbury,
Devon 1907
59405

and down to their cottages and to the tiny harbour far below. Roy Fisher was uncle and godfather to Jonathan Rowe, who still works in the post office at the top of the hill.

The people of Clovelly and all those living in remote country areas have Queen Victoria to thank for their daily deliver, for in 1897, to mark her Diamond Jubilee, the right of delivery was extended to every household in Britain. It was not long before the country postman assumed the position of influence he has never forfeited: he was universal confidante, social worker, message taker, welcome conduit for

local news and gossip - as well as being deliverer of the mails. There was little he did not know - or probably pass on - about the houses and occupants on his daily round. He trudged miles along puddled farm tracks carrying his heavy sack, then very often began another day's work; he might be a cobbler, able to take advantage of his round to collect and deliver repairs.

In the photograph of Countisbury (OPPOSITE PAGE, BELOW), along the coast from Clovelly, the Lynmouth postman has toiled a mile and a half up the one-in-four hill from the village below. He may have just enjoyed a brief respite at the Blue Ball Inn in the background. Now elderly, and with a long white beard, he might reminisce about his first years in the job when his sack would not be bulging as it is in the picture. It was in the 1880s that his work load increased dramatically - for after this time the souvenir postcard became very popular. The railways had made it possible for ordinary people to enjoy holidays and days out at the seaside, and sending souvenir cards to friends and family (at half the letter rate) became common practice. In addition, parcel post was introduced in 1883, and his sack and cart would have been swelled by books, newspapers and other goods. Country people quickly took to a service that they had been deprived of for so long.

The Houghton postman (OPPOSITE PAGE, TOP) is not a shining example of dress elegance. His crumpled tunic and baggy trousers have suffered the ill effects of wind and rain, and are soiled from the continual dust thrown up by passing horse traffic. He has his peaked shako to keep the weather from his head, but he does not benefit from the waterproof cape that was enjoyed by his metropolitan colleagues. It is hard to find a smart country postman from this era in the entire Frith archive, so there cannot have been many staff inspections. Yet the Post Office prided itself on the splendour of its uniforms. In 1872 its letter carriers were issued with smart navy blue tunics buttoned down the front and with red stand-up collars. Winter trousers were blue, and in the summer months these were replaced by a grey pair with red piping down the seams. The reason for the uniform was purely practical: letter boys of earlier years were continually robbed, as were the mail stages, so guards were deliberately clothed in military-style uniforms

Left:
Transferring the Mail Bags, Ruan Minor, Cornwall c1910 R65021

Below:
The Post Office, North Wootton, Norfolk 1908 60035

to discourage thieves. Early uniforms were bright scarlet, which showed every speck of mud, and it was not long before the Post Office changed to a more practical colour.

Before letters could be delivered they first had to be transported from the regional sorting offices and depots. In towns the Post Office had its own fleets of liveried vehicles. In the photograph of Ruan Minor in the remote far west of Cornwall (PREVIOUS PAGE), the mail bags are being transferred from a motorised van to a simple cart hauled by a lean, disinterested donkey. It is unlikely that that the vehicle is an official post van, for the driver is wearing a peaked cap: these were not introduced until 1932. More probably the photograph shows a carrier, who collected the local bags from town under contract. As well as running errands and offering lifts to villagers, he would carry the mails to the local postmen.

The village shop normally took on the role of post office in rural areas - the photograph of Compton Post Office in Surrey (BELOW) is a classic example. Some post offices were more modest than others: North Wootton, Norfolk (PREVIOUS PAGE), shown in 1908, is not exactly an advertisement for the Royal Mail's technological progress. However, we are assured that Mr and Mrs Raines ran an efficient service from this shed at the bottom of their garden. On the left is the slot through which senders poked their letters. The village was small in the days before the Great War, with just four large families and a dozen cottages. As it grew, so did the amount of daily post. Sometime in the late forties the hut burst at the seams - the queues for stamps must have stretched round and round the garden at Christmas time - and the operation was moved to a building in the main street. For a while chickens were kept in the old post shed, until it finally rotted away, neglected and forgotten.

Below:
The Post Office, Compton, Surrey 1906
55102

Pooter's Busy World

LONDON LIFE FOR THE VICTORIAN OFFICE WORKER

THE PICTURES BELOW show the heart of London's Square Mile in 1897 - the Royal Exchange with Threadneedle Street behind, and the Bank of England and Threadneedle Street. Richard Jefferies describes the frenetic scene in his 1883 book 'The Story of My Heart':

Like the spokes of a wheel converging, streams of human life flow into this agitated pool of blue carts and yellow omnibuses, varnished carriages and brown vans ... men and women fill the interstices between the carriages and blacken the surface, till the vans almost float on human beings ... this is the vortex and whirlpool, the centre of human life today on the earth. Here it seethes and whirls, not for an hour only, but for all present time, hour by hour, day by day, year by year.

Right:
The Bank of
England,
London 1890
L130179

Below:
The Royal
Exchange,
London 1890
L130208

City life seems as frantic in the 1890s as it does today: the bowler-hatted man in the foreground (OVERLEAF) is dashing from the Bank of England to his office with the latest figures (there were no faxes in Victoria's day). The streets teem with people, and judging by the packed top deck on the left there were never enough London buses to go round. The 1881 census revealed a steady rise in the size of the professional, commercial and managerial classes: Britain was no longer the sole powerhouse of world industry, and the early prosperity of Victoria's reign had dissipated.

In 1890, the City's fortunes were founded not on industrial might but on the precarious realm of international finance. London in the 1890s had become the world of the salary earner, of banking, insurance and shipping. London was now the banking capital of the world, with overseas investment rising to a colossal two billion pounds. Another Victorian writer, Charles Dickens, wrote in 'Our Mutual Friend': 'O mighty Shares, Relieve us of our money, scatter it for us, buy us and sell us!'

At the lower end of the employment scale, making your way was a struggle. If you were hard-working, you might be made a senior clerk in a bank or insurance office after years of loyal service. Job mobility was unheard of, and staying with the same employer was the only chance of financial security and a modest pension. You would start at seven in the morning, and complaints about the poor light or bad air would be frowned upon. Even the union failed to improve working conditions.

The best way to climb the ladder was to specialise and become a ledger or a billing clerk. But it was wise to watch your back, for young girls were taking over the office desks, and typing-pools were being set up in the offices of mutual insurance companies and brokers (the typewriter first appeared in the 1880s, replacing the quill pen).

George Pooter, that quintessentially ordinary Londoner, gives us a crystal-clear picture of 1890s city life in Grossmith's 'Diary of a Nobody', which was published originally in the popular magazine 'Punch'. He proudly reported to his wayward son Lupin: 'My boy, after 21 years of industry and strict attention to the interests of my superiors, I have now been rewarded with the position of Senior Clerk and a salary increase of £100'. Unimpressed, his son informed him that after five days in his new job and with no attention at all to the interests of his superiors, he had made £200 - on a risky share deal.

Right:
Queen Victoria Street,
London 1897
L130055

The Constant Struggle

Lives of the London street traders

Below:
Chimney Sweep,
London 1884
L130115

THE STREETS OF LONDON were thick with beggars and confidence tricksters. In the 1880s 300,000 Londoners were classified as poor. Many beggars made desperate efforts to lift themselves and their families out of their unrelenting poverty by taking on a trade, however small and insignificant. They were reluctant to apply for Outdoor Relief under the Poor Law. The match sellers, shoe blacks and flower girls, very often displaced from the countryside where life was yet more unendurable, were given short shrift by many of the great and wealthy. An 1888 tourist guidebook suggested the following evasive action be taken by travellers: 'To get rid of your beggar, when wearisome, take no notice of him at all. He will only follow you till you meet a more likely person, but no farther'.

Street traders faced suspicion from the public and persecution by the police on a daily basis. Their lives were a constant struggle to win food and shelter; many lived in cheap, crowded lodging houses in poor areas of the West End and the City, where they were preyed upon mercilessly by voracious landlords. There was, of course, no social relief, and families were forced back on their own cunning and guile to keep body and soul together.

The Victorian social critic Henry Mayhew reported that the *Chimney Sweeps* (LEFT) were a tight-knit community, and that Master sweepers often let rooms to families in the same trade. The climbing boys, often from the Workhouse, earned 2d or 3d a day, but were sometimes given an extra 6d by grateful householders. They climbed easily up through wide flues using their elbows, but often found themselves stuck and near-suffocated in narrow nine-inch chimneys. For young children it must have been the most terrifying experience. George Smart's invention of the familiar set of hollow rods topped with a broad bristle brush encouraged an end to the cruelty, and an Act of Parliament finally made child sweeps illegal in 1875.

A *Chair Mender* (ABOVE RIGHT) squats in the passage outside the kitchen of a London house. There were once 2,500 cabinet-making shops in London, many employing children. When powered sawmills and mechanical production methods brought ready-made furniture onto the market, many thousands of craftsmen lost their jobs. Here, an old man re-canes a child's chair. The house-keeper maintains a wary eye.

The old *Ginger-Cake Seller* with his laden tray (RIGHT) stands in the gutter of King Street, Greenwich near the entrance to the park. His dark-coloured cake of flour, treacle and ground ginger was a favourite snack with Victorians at fairs and street events. The roughly-shaped pieces were measured into paper cones and topped with a blanched almond. This old man's gingercake was probably made by his wife or daugh-ters. His laden tray has seen better days and the strap has been given makeshift repairs on more than one occasion. The old man's foot rests on what is probably the tray cover, which is gathering dust in the road.

Sporting their red uniforms, the

Above:
**Chair Mender
1877
L130112**

Right:
**Ginger Cake
Seller 1884
L130111**

Bootblack Boys (OPPOSITE PAGE) were a familiar sight on the streets of London. The bootblack business grew into a highly-organised and philanthropic affair: the Ragged Schools, Saffron Hill, set up the first society, and nine others followed. Their aim was to educate orphan boys and to give them a good start in the world and, by the 1880s, the shoeblack societies had four hundred boys on their books. Members of the Shoeblack Brigade were licensed to trade by the Metropolitan Police and carried on their business unhindered.

Small children cluster round the *Hokey-Pokey Stall* (ABOVE RIGHT) licking at the cheap ice cream. They look like ragged street urchins in their rumpled suits and battered boots, and were probably bought their penny treats in return for posing for the photographer. The stallholder, standing in apron and straw hat, is no more than a youth, and is probably one of many hired hands working for a much larger concern.

A young *Match Seller* (RIGHT) poses for the photographer. Selling a few lucifers was all too often the pretext for begging. This tiny waif is offering boxes of Bryant and May's fusee 'Alpine Vesuvian' matches, popularly known as Brimstones. His job was hardly a desirable one, but he was considerably better off than those poor Londoners who were involved in the manufacturing of matches: the yellow phosphorus used in the process caused a debilitating disease of the mouth known as 'Phossy Jaw'.

Bryant and May employed seven hundred girls in their match factories. In 1888 these girls went on strike for better pay and conditions, but such a protest and threat to public order was rare amongst workers in Victorian Britain.

Opposite page:
**The Shoeblack
1895**
L130114

Above right:
**Hokey-Pokey
Stall, Greenwich
1884**
L130110

Right:
**The Young Match
Seller 1884**
L130116

A Stately Pleasure Dome Decreed

THE CRYSTAL PALACE - JOSEPH PAXTON'S SEVEN-DAY WONDER FOR THE WORKING MAN

JOSEPH PAXTON designed the Crystal Palace in seven days. When it was first built in Hyde Park for the 1851 Great Exhibition it was over 600 yards long and 150 yards wide. At that time glass was unheard-of as a building material. The 2,000 workers who erected it at high speed bolted and welded together 3,300 iron columns, 205 miles of sash-bars and 293,655 panes of glass. With its lofty central transept and colossal glass elevations, it was built to impress.

It had been created for the world to wonder at, as a temple containing the triumphs of Victorian art and industry. The original conception had been Prince Albert's, who was President of the Royal Society of Arts; he believed a showcase of the varied technological and artistic achievements of the many countries of the civilised world would stimulate international trade.

Inside were galleries offering eight miles of display space that was occupied by 14,000 exhibitors from Britain, the United States and most European nations. E F Benson describes a selection of the exhibits in his life of Queen Victoria: 'machinery and oil-yielding palms, stuffed elephants with immense ivory tusks, locomotives, stamps for crushing ores, the pit head of a coal mine, Persian carpets, Kidderminster rugs, porcelain and wax flowers and glass paper weights and bedsteads and blankets'.

Over six million people visited the exhibition between May and October 1851. The emerging middle classes were captivated: here they saw novelties and inventions that would enrich their lives, made possible by the new techniques of mass production.

After the Exhibition, it was decided to move the Crystal Palace to another site, and to turn it into a temple of leisure. For London's millions the Crystal Palace brought opportunities for exciting excursions and days out. If the original building in Hyde Park had been spectacular, it was even more so when it was re-erected in the wooded parkland of Sydenham in south-east London: the original three-storey building was enlarged to five storeys, making it almost half as big again.

It was filled with an abundance of

Below:
The Crystal
Palace, London
1890
C207020

Opposite:
The Interior
Galleries c1886
C207992

Grecian, Roman, Chinese, Egyptian and other displays, lavish in both size and scope. The grounds were transformed into fantastic gardens with many flower temples, pleasure walks, fountains and lakes; there were statues, urns, busts, temples and miniature palaces to delight the artistic eye and to stimulate civic sensibility. Its impact on the London working man and his family must have been extraordinary: most were used to living in considerable poverty, in cramped tenements and slums where sunlight rarely penetrated.

Brunel constructed water towers three hundred feet high (CENTRE RIGHT) which held almost half a million gallons of water to serve the complex system of fountains; there were lakes, islands, a maze, a grotto, groves, temples and lawns. It became a paradise of leisure for Londoners, who flocked to enjoy the special displays and exhibitions.

There were firework displays by Messrs Brock that lit up the London sky with flights of 5,000 rockets, celestial cascades and plumes of fire; a fiery Battle of Jutland was played out in the sky before thousands; Blondin walked the high wire and cooked an omelette seventy feet up in the air.

Queen Victoria invited everyone to see her Palace, including the Shah of Persia. Like her subjects, she was delighted by it. The Palace was an unparalleled symbol of the continuing glories and achievements of her reign.

Londoners were shocked in 1936 when the building was destroyed by fire. The deep red corona could be seen in the sky from all over the city. Crowds flocked to watch the spectacle, at once horrified and fascinated. No public building since has approached the Crystal Palace for sheer splendour.

Top:
The Lake,
The Crystal
Palace 1890
L130060

Centre:
The Crystal
Palace 1900
L130147

Below:
The Park,
The Crystal
Palace 1890
L130021

The OK Thing to Do

THE EARLY YEARS OF REGENT'S PARK ZOO

FOUNDED BY the Zoological Society of London in grounds laid out by the architect Decimus Burton, the Regent's Park Zoo opened its doors to the public in 1828. Early visitors were confronted for the first time with exotic bears, kangaroos, zebras, llamas and an ostrich. It seems odd to us today that the public were encouraged to feed them: there was a stall selling cakes, fruits and nuts. Thirty thousand Londoners visited in the first six months.

The walks and promenades soon became a parade for fashionable London, and the zoo was familiarly known as 'the most delightful lounge in the metropolis'. Animal care being in its infancy, there were often unfortunate confrontations between beasts and humans: ladies who thoughtlessly poked their parasols through the bars of the monkey cage found their veils and dresses ripped and gashed by paws

Left:
Bactrian Camel, Regent's Park, London 1913
65251

Below:
Pelicans, Regent's Park 1913
65252

thrust back at them. On hot Bank Holidays the stench from the many cages could be overwhelming. In 1840, a kangaroo escaped, causing havoc as it hopped energetically amongst the

throngs of panicking visitors.

The zoo had Indian elephants from the very beginning. It was one old woman's job to sell buns and cakes to feed them. The zoo resisted appeals that their keepers should wear exotic Asian costume to add to the spectacle, but the elephants were permitted to give rides to children, who clambered excitedly up specially-built staircases and clung precariously to the howdah, which was filled to bursting. In early days the money for the rides went to the keeper in the form of tips. One favourite of the London public, Jumbo, who was at the zoo during the 1870s and 80s, earned a creditable £600 a year for his labours.

There was always a conflict between education and entertainment - the Victorians were particularly fascinated by the exotic and freakish - and the authorities had to battle to maintain the zoo's prime function, which was as an educational institution.

Advertising for zoos at the time was often little more than a succession of fairground-style hyperbole: 'our elephant runs faster than a racehorse, is able to drink forty buckets of water a day or the same quantity of beer, and if fed on bread alone his daily intake would be enough for a working man for two years'. The animals quickly caught the public imagination and were often caricatured in 'Punch' and in music-hall songs. One refrain by The Great Vance went: 'Walking in the zoo is the OK thing to do.'

The March of the Multiples

THE GRADUAL DEMISE OF THE SMALL CORNER SHOP

DOWN THE CENTURIES the British people had made every attempt to be self-sufficient. The landed classes relied on their extensive home farms and kitchen gardens to keep them supplied with poultry, meat and vegetables, and they kept servants to carry out a whole range of services like shoe repair. The poor had little spare money to spend in shops, and preferred to haggle over local produce in street markets, where traders were as keen to sell as they were to buy. The photograph of Ormskirk market (BELOW) shows a scene familiar in towns all over the country at this time. Market culture was boisterous, bustling and essentially good-natured. Here the working-class housewife with a tiny income could haggle for as long as she wished to find a bargain.

Behind the stalls and awnings there was a very different story. Here were the small town shops, the baker, tailor and shoe repairer, businesses that were precarious and uncertain. The corner shop, like the tiny one pictured in the

Below:
**Market Place,
Ormskirk,
Lancashire 1892**
34137

Right:
Corner Shop,
The Old Rectory,
York 1909
61864

Below:
Jermyn and Perry
the Draper's,
King's Lynn,
Norfolk 1908
60023

city of York (LEFT), battled to survive, for it was in direct competition with the market on the far side of the pavement. Unlike the market traders, this modest shopkeeper had considerable fixed costs, for he had invested in premises and in a bigger stock for which he had had to pay cash. It is hardly surprising that he was impoverished and more than a little frustrated with his lot. This tiny shop was once the Rectory, and clearly has a minimal space available for display. Shops like this might see no more than a dozen customers a day, and were often run by widows, struggling to pay the rent to the landlord as well as suppliers' bills.

The more substantial small town shops relied on the carriage trade for their business. Shopkeepers would doff their hats to the local Lord, but would bend double if his footman's gig drew up alongside the premises - for he was the one who controlled the substantial household budget. Pursuing a new account could be a long and arduous campaign, and winning one a major victory. Yet such desirable business had its drawbacks: the landed classes would not dream of paying cash to suppliers, with the direct consequence that many small shopkeepers found themselves hopelessly extended and at the mercy of their bank. Running a successful and

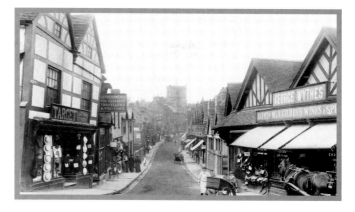

expanding shop required capital, plus the will to invest and take a risk. Many shops shied away from the fight, and stayed uneasily on the fringes, unable to buy goods at advantageous prices from wholesalers or offer an attractive enough product range to potential clients.

By the 1890s a much more serious development was threatening the livelihoods of the small town shopkeeper. Since the 1870s there had been a huge increase in the number of multiples who were setting up shop in the high street. These 'company shops', like Liptons, Boots and Home & Colonial, had the financial muscle and aggression to offer branded goods at rock-bottom prices. They sold on a cash basis only, and quickly began to win customers from the smaller independents.

Working class shoppers were targeted in particular, for they were satisfied with the 'cheap and cheerful' if it saved them precious pennies - the less they had to pay out the less they had to earn. The multiples' retail philosophy was profoundly simple: small profits and quick returns.

To survive, the independents were forced to be modern and progressive. They took over adjacent shop premises

Above:
High Street, Droitwich, Worcestershire 1904
51938

from ailing competitors, and invested in staff and prestigious shop fronts. Jermyn and Perry the draper's shop in King's Lynn (PREVIOUS PAGE) has invested a considerable amount of money in setting out its stall. The splendid gilded glass sign, the distinctive decorative lamps overhanging the pavement, the broad glass windows that offer scope for innovative marketing and display - all these reveal a keenness to compete and a will to succeed. Window display was in its infancy in this era, and novices at the art often crammed every available inch of window space with stock.

When window space was restricted many shops took over the pavement. In Leominster (BELOW), Plumber's the hardware shop have obscured their window with a huge display of rakes and garden tools. It was crude but effective. Yet this ploy had its dangers: more sophisticated customers often felt such lavish displays bordered on vulgarity, and were

repelled by the mob of 'street urchins' that invariably hung around outside. Note the children on the pavement outside Jermyn and Perry's. The two shop staff are keeping a wary eye on them.

Competing with the multiples became the preoccupation of the independent Edwardian shopkeepers. Unable to sell to the working people, they turned back to the customers they had failed to win before - the 'better classes', who were now supplemented by the burgeoning managerial and professional classes, making a much broader and more substantial target. Product choice became the order of the day, and shops were soon offering a bewildering range of products - there were, for instance, 360 types of biscuit available in 1900, made by household names like Peek Frean, McVitie and Huntley and Palmer. An independent grocer stocked as many biscuit brands as he could and made a virtue of it. The shopkeepers' advertising of this era reveals their desperation to entice and attract the sophisticated new client. In Arnold Bennett's 'The Old Wives' Tale', published in 1908, Mr Povey the draper attaches considerable importance to his window tickets: 'There were heavy oblong tickets for flannels, shirting and other stuffs ... diamond shaped tickets for bonnets, gloves and flimflams ... The words 'lasting', 'durable', 'unshrinkable', 'latest', 'cheap', 'stylish', novelty', 'choice', 'tasteful' exhausted the entire possible vocabulary of tickets. He dreamed of other tickets, in original shapes, with original legends ...' Shops extended their range of services, too, offering daily deliveries and free advice about cooking and the preparation of various foods. This was the era of the delivery boy with his bicycle and pannier.

Below:
High Street,
Leominster,
Herefordshire
1904
51920

The retail pattern had been set for good. The picture of Harrow-on-the-Hill in 1914 (ABOVE) shows the character of the British shopping street that was to prevail for decades. On the left is Home & Colonial, which by this date had several hundred branches. Their pricing policy was aggressive: signs in the window proclaim '2d in the shilling returned'. Two doors along is Boots, 'the largest chemist in the world' - Jesse Boot had come a long way from plain pharmacy, and was now offering a bewildering range of fancy goods and stationery. Three doors along from Boots is Sainsbury's, with its distinctive shop interiors, spacious, practical and hygenic, worlds away from the small, cramped corner shop in York.

The era of the small general shop was almost over. Its customers had deserted it, either for cheaper prices or a wider range of goods, and an era in retailing was near its end. The multiples were winning. Unassailable, they either forced the smaller independents out of business or absorbed and rebranded them. Jermyn and Perry, the Kings Lynn drapers, were eventually taken over by Debenhams. It was a process that was repeated in every high street in the country.

Above:
Station Road, Harrow-on-the-Hill, Middlesex 1914
66820

Mr Lawrence's Soap, Lavender and Leeches

YE OLDEST CHYMIST SHOPPE IN ENGLAND

THE ANTIQUE-LETTERED signboard over the shop in the photograph announces that it is 'Ye Oldest Chymist Shoppe in England, Established 1720'. After more than two hundred and fifty years of dispensing medicines to the people of Knaresborough, it closed for business just two years ago.

Our picture shows the old shop in 1911, when the apothecary was Mr Lawrence. His family had been selling patent liniments and corn eradicators in the picturesque Yorkshire town of Knaresborough for two generations.

Inside, we can see the various pestles and mortars in which he ground his potions and medicines. The giant pestle with its marble mortar was turned by dogs in a cage until 1840. Behind is Mr Lawrence's 'bleeding couch', where he pulled teeth - possibly a little too public an exhibition for modern tastes. Today we prefer to suffer in private. Many of the glass-stoppered drug bottles on the shelves and the spectacular bottle tree on the counter have been preserved.

Lawrence's was noted by the discerning for its Knaresborough Old English

Below:
The Old Chemist's Shop, Knaresborough, Yorkshire 1911
63543

Lavender Water, which was sold in the fancy cut-glass bottles on the counter on the right. The special lavender water is still a much sought-after gift item, packaged in wicker-covered bottles.

On the counters and shelves are early Box Brownie cameras, boxes of Colgate dental cream, oatmeal soap, aromatic pine inhalations, numerous packets of pills, potions and cures, retorts, scales and weights, and shaving brushes for gentlemen. Mr Lawrence's leech jar has been preserved.

The fine old shop front remains almost unchanged, and Mr Lawrence's brass plate is still in position. Mrs Dorothy Merrin ran the shop until recently and did a brisk trade in his patent Pino-Creo Inhalent and Corn and Wart Eradicator.

The premises are now in the ownership of Pickles', the town manufacturers of foot ointments, and they offer high quality toffees and a range of creams and insect repellants from the old chemist's shop.

Below:
The Interior of the Old Chemist's Shop, Knaresborough 1914
67279

Bad Manners in the High Street

Right:
The Oldest House, Frome, Somerset 1907
58851

Below:
Parliament Street, Harrogate, Yorkshire 1907
58649

THE BATTLE OF THE SIGNS AMONGST VICTORIAN AND EDWARDIAN SHOPKEEPERS

THE GEORGIANS were renowned for their architecture: think of the flowing crescents of Bath or the mellow terraces of a town like Harrogate. Their shops, too, normally modest in size, had frontages that were in harmony with the buildings alongside. A Georgian high street is almost always a study in good taste.

It is regrettable that the Georgians' good manners were rarely displayed in the Victorian era. In Frith photographs of the 1890s and 1900s, the high street

Above:
**Fore Street,
Taunton,
Somerset 1902**
48723

becomes an arena for pitched battles between warring shopkeepers. The weapons are not picks and shovels - although one often feels if they could have used them they would - but letters and signs. The photograph of Frome (OPPOSITE) depicts the quintessential small corner shop, almost cloying in its quaintness. Mr Hughes's shop name is painted discreetly above the door and there are modest Rowntree's Cocoa logos on the windows. Yet even Mr Hughes could not resist the lure of a sizeable but unnecessary 'Grape-Nuts' enamel sign which he has placed high up on his wall, well outside the fascia of his shop. Today we find these old signs nostalgic and fascinating, yet they were the thin end of a very large wedge from which we have been suffering ever since.

In the picture of Harrogate (OPPOSITE), Boots the cash chemist's have installed their standard gilded wooden sign over their premises, which smothers the entire frontage from the roof downwards. Boots, it would appear, were determined to make an impact in the town. Opposite, Mr Taylor the chemist has risen to the challenge and has fought back with an even more gigantic sign with letters that would have each required three men to lift. The effect is the equivalent of having both managers standing facing each other on their respective pavements, screaming their sales messages through megaphones from dawn to dusk - for that they would be arrested, and quite properly. Yet they were permitted to assault us visually and no-one could say a word.

In 1902 in Taunton (ABOVE), The Stores, not content with cladding their building with fake timbering, have turned it into a gigantic and boisterous

Above:
**Market Place,
Stamford,
Lincolnshire 1922**
72298

hoarding, a forty-foot street poster. Poor Mr Spiller's sign on the tiny shop next door is no bigger than The Stores' 'Price List Free' sign over the entrance. Once the process of gigantism was set in motion it was almost impossible to reverse - who would make the first move, you or your competitor? In Stamford in 1922 (ABOVE), Freeman, Hardy and Willis, not content with emblazoning their name over their own shop, have invaded the houses next door. The people of Stamford must have ended up with eye-strain.

Modern research has proved that the battle of the signs was all in vain, and that any victory achieved was a Pyrrhic one. Tests have shown that shoppers rarely look up at any sign above the level of the shop window, for the view-

ing angle is too acute. In most town high streets it is impossible to step back far enough to read such massive letters without being run down by a car. It has also been proved that a tiny two-inch letter can be read perfectly well from across the street and that the most effective signs are those at eye-level.

Such signs, it seems, were money wasted. But they clearly demonstrate the war that developed in the retail trade after the multiples moved into our towns near the end of the 19th century. It is a war that has never stopped being fought, for there are as many examples of excessive signage today as there were a hundred years ago.

Many of us would welcome a return to the more sedate and better-mannered Georgian times.

Trading Under the Clock

THE LONG WAIT FOR HALIFAX'S MAGNIFICENT BOROUGH MARKET

HALIFAX had been a market town for many centuries, but unlike its close neighbours Bradford and Huddersfield, it had never enjoyed the benefits of a covered market hall. A Market Act in 1810 prohibited street trading, and anyone caught selling goods from a basket around the town could be arrested. A custom-built market hall had become a pressing priority.

The Town Council had been buying and setting aside land for such a scheme since the 1850s, but building did not actually begin until 1891. The design of the market was put out to competition, and the winning architects were Joseph and John Leeming of London, both Halifax-born.

The new Borough Market was to be the magnificent centre-piece of the town and was eagerly awaited. Construction, however, progressed at a

Left:
The Entrance
and Arcade,
Borough Market,
Halifax, Yorkshire
1896
38777

painfully slow pace, and the Council was obliged to provide extra injections of funds more than once. The building was finally completed in 1896 at a total cost of £130,000.

On 25 July 1896 the grand opening ceremony was carried out by the Duke and Duchess of York, who addressed the packed hall from below the imposing ornamental clock.

Historian Eric Webster has described the Borough Market's jubilant medley of architectural styles: 'Flemish gables, Florentine palazzo windows and baroque thin turrets ... all blend together into a building of character'. It was indeed a splendid construction, built mainly in local stone, and entered through magnificent ornamental iron doors created by William MacFarlane of Glasgow.

The market was set on a sloping site, and around its heavily rusticated perimeter walls were forty-three small shops, originally all butchers. Inside, arranged in straight lines, were twenty small shop units and thirty-three stalls that on market days could accommodate almost a hundred traders.

Sixty feet overhead, supported on decorative iron pillars, was a spectacular octagonal dome of glass and iron. Directly below it was the renowned ornamental clock that soon became a favourite meeting point for visiting shoppers, and which was once visible from any point in the hall.

Would-be market traders could rent stalls weekly for between half a crown and eight shillings, and the shops in the arcades cost £100 per year. The fish market was originally in the main hall, but it was soon agreed by one and all that it would be better sited outside in Albion Street.

Right:
The Interior Hall, Borough Market, Halifax 1896
38782

Carrying Water,
Shottery,
Warwickshire c1890
S297546

Well, Windlass, Bucket and Gossip

THE DAILY COUNTRYSIDE TASK OF FETCHING WATER FROM WELL OR STREAM

Below:
Carrying Water,
Shottery,
Warwickshire
c1890
S297545

FOR TOWN DWELLERS with mains taps it is almost impossible to understand the countryman's preoccupation with water.

If he has a well he will watch it like a hawk, endlessly checking the level, watching the sky for rain, recalling with neighbours infamous droughts and the pattern of precipitation throughout each and every year. Some might think him obsessed. In very dry country areas, water is almost a form of currency, with water-rich villagers looking at less fortunate neighbours with a mixture of pity and scorn. Most people in towns think of prolonged periods of rain as an irritation. The countryman, however, looks on such downpours philosophically, saying, 'Ah, good for the well!'

Collecting water is one of the most ancient jobs known to man. Buckets and yokes were used in prehistoric times and were still being used by the Victorians. Going to the stream was a daily task for cottagers. In the picture of Shottery (LEFT) we see girls dipping their buckets in the placid flow. By using a yoke it was possible to carry several gallons at a time, for the buckets are held high and the weight spread across the shoulders. Holding them by hand made them bang awkwardly against thighs or knees. Each girl had to make several journeys a day down to the stream, and more on washing day.

Carrying the buckets was hard work, especially after a day spent working in the fields, with a trek home at the day's end of two or more miles. If the stream was at the other end of the village there was yet more carrying involved. The girls' pinafores are unnaturally white and immaculate, suggesting that the Frith photographer has carefully posed them in their Sunday best.

Going for water was considered 'ooman's work' (woman's work). Flora Thompson, in 'Lark Rise to Candleford' recounts how many villagers felt that if a woman made her husband go for water it was a 'sin and a shame'. One reason for this view could be that the women enjoyed going for water because it gave them the opportunity to meet with their friends. While they queued they could indulge in a bout of good old-fashioned gossip. The task might have been onerous, but at least it had its compensations.

Top:
**The Water-Seller,
Haslemere, Surrey
1888**
H35501

Right:
**The Mill,
Mapledurham,
Oxfordshire 1890**
27091

The water-seller was a regular caller at many dry, heathland villages, where water was at a premium. In the picture of Haslemere (OPPOSITE PAGE, TOP LEFT) he is filling a cottager's bucket with water from his barrel. Millponds were another important source of water in the village. At Mapledurham (OPPOSITE PAGE, BOTTOM LEFT), a carter is filling his barrel while his horse cools its feet in the shallows.

More fortunate villagers had their own well. At Whitmore Vale Farm, near Grayshott in Hampshire (RIGHT), two women are filling the buckets. One turns the windlass and the other waits with her little boy, ready to carry the overflowing buckets back to the farmhouse. The bucket at the end of the rope will have a stone in the bottom so that it sinks easily. The parrot in the cage is enjoying the spectacle.

It has been pointed out how curious it was that Jack and Jill went up a hill to fetch a pail of water. Most wells lie on low ground, and it was the job of the skilled water-diviner to find a reliable source. This age-old technique employs nothing more than a forked stick, and has not been superseded by modern technology. Everyone hired the diviner, even those who were the most sceptical about the realms of the unknown and the spiritual. Wells could be a hundred feet deep, others mere scratchings in the ground: every country area had its own unique geology, and the depth and amount of water differed significantly over a patch of ground a hundred yards wide. If a well did start to run dry and the owner brought in the well-digger, it could lead to serious disputes: nothing incensed a villager more than the belief that his neighbour was stealing his water by diverting the underground streams.

Turning on a tap hardly offers you the time or opportunity to think. Yet when you turn the handle of an old windlass and watch the bucket slowly descend into the darkness it can lead you into a quiet world of meditation and reflection.

Some would go further and say that having a well seems to encourage the philosophical frame of mind in man. Rider Haggard, author and farmer, reports that when he was digging out a deep, disused well in his native Norfolk he came upon sea sand and thousands of shells lining the bottom. It led him to reflect on the distant origins of man and the planet, and how 'in some dim age the sea once rolled' a hundred feet below the present level of the earth.

Below:
The Well,
Whitmore Vale
Farm, Grayshott,
Hampshire 1917
67934

Too Proud for Charity

Above:
Gardening at the King Edward VII Sanatorium, Midhurst, Sussex 1907
58337

Right:
Gardening at the King Edward VII Sanatorium, Midhurst, Sussex 1907
58337a

KING EDWARD VII'S MISSION TO RELIEVE THE SUFFERING OF TUBERCULOSIS PATIENTS

IN 1903 King Edward VII visited Bavaria and was much impressed by the fine sanatoria he saw, and by the high quality of care provided for patients suffering from tuberculosis. He knew he would not find anything comparable in his own country. On his return he spoke to the financier Sir Ernest Cassel, and persuaded him to fund the building of a similar sanatorium in Britain. The scheme was aimed specifically at 'the poorer middle classes', who had nowhere to go for treatment, for they were 'too proud to avail themselves of public charity'.

A breezy site facing south was found high up on the Downs at Midhurst in Sussex. The King announced an open competition to find an innovative design for the buildings, and it was won by Percy Adams, whose plan was in the style of Edwin Lutyens.

The pioneering gardener Gertrude Jekyll, who had cooperated with Lutyens himself on many schemes, lived just a few miles away at Munstead, and when she heard about the sanatorium she was keen to be involved. Percy Adams had set aside 152 acres of land for the grounds; assisted by two local gardeners, Miss Jekyll began laying out a formal garden. There were lawns, paths and a number of walks created especially for the patients - measured exercise was an important part of their rehabilitation. Miss Jekyll paid for many of the plants used out of her own pocket, so enthusiastic was she for the success of the project. She built terraces separated by low stone walls, and laid out beds containing aromatic herbs, flowers and shrubs.

The patients worked in the gardens planting, hoeing and weeding, and clearly enjoyed their labours, as the two Frith photographs show. The sunlight and clean air aided their recovery, and Miss Jekyll's scheme proved an immense success. The sanatorium gained a reputation as a pioneering establishment for the alleviation and cure of tuberculosis, and led the way in new treatments.

By the 1960s the disease had been almost eradicated. By supplemental Royal Charter the sanatorium was renamed the King Edward VII Hospital, and it changed its role to that of an acute hospital, treating both public and private patients.

The beautiful gardens had by this time deteriorated; the Honourable Lady Barttelot agreed to take over the reins, and she has worked resolutely ever since to restore them to Gertrude Jekyll's original planting plan.

Below:
Weeding the Jekyll Flower beds, King Edward VII Sanatorium, Midhurst 1907
58334

An Eye for a Bargain

JOSTLING FOR CHUTNEY AT BARNSTAPLE'S PANNIER MARKET

IN the dim light is a sea of hats, caps and upturned faces. Business at the Barnstaple Pannier Market has been suspended for a few moments for the Frith photographer. As soon as he steps down from his platform the bargaining will begin again in earnest.

Everyone in North Devon seems to have turned out: even the curate is there in the thick of the throng, searching for his favourite chutney.

Barnstaple Pannier Market was built in 1855. Its spectacular, lofty wooden vaulted roof is cathedral-like, exalting the proceedings below. On the fringes of the crowd stand the stall-holders - farmers' wives, country women and old men. For most, the shillings earned were a vital part of their survival, but for some the sale of a few vegetables and fruits helped pay the cost of tobacco and beer.

On the left is a woman in a white blouse and apron standing guard by her pannier basket. She would have been up before dawn, filling it with jars of home-made jams and marmalade, and with cabbages and cucumbers fresh-picked from her garden. Then there was the long journey on the carrier's cart through the twisting Devon lanes into town.

Inside the market building each stall-holder had a numbered pitch. The cost of a year's stall rent in 1919 was just 6d. Today it is considerably more, but the Barnstaple Market Superintendant believes it is still a bargain, for on Tuesdays, Fridays and Saturdays the hall is filled, and you can pick over the produce of 400 stalls. Prices are low, and shoppers discover produce they would not find in High Street shops, such as rare cottage garden plants and forgotten varieties of apple.

The 1903 picture (BELOW) shows the cavernous room in the afternoon after everyone has packed up and gone home. There seems to be an atmosphere of shell-shock. Two old men rest their arthritic joints on the bench on the left, and the stragglers clear their stalls. It is a welcome calm after the storm.

Left:
The Pannier Market,
Barnstaple, Devon 1919
69324

Right:
The Pannier Market,
Barnstaple 1903
49622

From Anvil to Petrol Pump

THE CHANGING ROLE OF THE VILLAGE BLACKSMITH

Left:
Samuel Govier's
Forge,
Lyme Regis,
Dorset 1909
61633a

IN THE early 1900s, no village was without its blacksmith's shop. The smith's main task was the shoeing of horses, but he turned his hand to a great variety of jobs that involved the working of metal.

Sturdy in physique and immensely strong, the smith was credited with mythical ancestry by the Romans, for he performed the alchemy of making hard metal flow into intricate shapes. The first smith was Vulcan, who forged Jupiter's thunderbolts.

The painter J M Whistler visited the fashionable seaside town of Lyme Regis in 1895. As he climbed the steep main street he must have heard Samuel Govier's hammer crashing against steel in his yard, and seen the glowing fire and the shower of incandescent sparks through the dim doorway. Captivated, he set to and painted 'The Master Smith of Lyme Regis', a fine portrait of Govier which now hangs in the Boston Museum. A painting by a famous artist is no guarantee of immortality, though. In Lyme today nothing of Govier remains, and where his smithy stood, and where the town children gathered to watch the steam hissing from the white-hot shoes, Woolworth's now stands. The Frith photograph (LEFT) shows Govier at work shoeing in 1909.

His assistant holds a rasp which is used for paring down and cleaning the horse's hoof. Against the wall on the right is the grindstone for sharpening tools.

In the picture of the Alderley Edge forge (BELOW), an apprentice in tattered leather apron is prising off a shoe from the foot of a farm horse. He has already cut off the nail-ends with a rasp. Though a kick from the animal could fatally injure him, the boy shows no fear of lifting the heavy foot. His progress is watched by the smith who is leaning against a barrel on the left. The Alderley smiths have been at work since six, stoking the fire inside the forge with the bellows, cutting shoe-length sections from metal bars and then heating them over the fire, and beating them into shape with a catshead hammer. The nail holes are punched through with a pritchell. Each horse had its own unique shoeing template, which the smith used to form shoes that would fit precisely. Many a half-tortured horse with hoof trouble was cured after passing through the village smithy. As well as being farriers, the Alderley Edge smiths fitted cartwheels with iron hoops for the wheelwright - in the background is a pile of wheel stocks.

The horse-shoe shaped doorway of the Merrow forge (OPPOSITE PAGE, RIGHT) was a tour-de-force of brickwork and would have cost the smith a large

Below:
The Village Smithy, Alderley Edge, Cheshire 1896
37477a

amount of money. That he could even contemplate such a lavish outlay reflects the amount of work there was for him in the early years of the 20th century. Everyone rode, and there were carriage horses, plough teams, hunters and ponies - all of which required re-shoeing every few weeks. In addition the Merrow smiths would have made hoes, repaired farm tools, sharpened scythes on the grindstone and mended kettles and pots for the housewives of the village. The horse being shod in the picture has travelled to the forge in a vehicle, for he is wearing knee boots to protect him from injury. He is clipped out and is probably a hunter - his owner has given him a rug to wear against the chill weather.

The second picture of the Merrow forge (BOTTOM RIGHT) reveals a startling change. Gone are the dusty yard and the scattered farm implements awaiting repair; instead there are petrol pumps. There is no horse in sight, and the old smith is being given his instructions by a liveried chauffeur. The smiths of Merrow are no longer farriers but mechanics, and they have learned the skills of motor vehicle repair. They have swapped their hammers and bellows for acetylene welding equipment. They had had little choice - with the coming of the car much of the smith's traditional business evaporated, and he had to adapt to survive. The horse shoe-shaped doorway is still in position, but it looks as if someone has made every attempt possible to obliterate the lettering. Today, there are no traces left of this picturesque old forge - the site is now occupied by a modern service station.

At the time of this photograph the Rural Industries Bureau was attempting to encourage a public taste for ornate

decorative ironwork. The smith had always carried out a certain amount of such work, but in most villages it was never a regular contributor to his income. Pattern books of the period reveal much use of iron gates and grilles in prestigious buildings, and some smiths were able to make the break from traditional smithing and specialise in architectural ironwork. It was a very

Above:
The Forge,
Merrow,
Surrey 1913
65231

Right:
The Petrol
Station, Merrow,
Surrey 1927
79918

fortunate development, for it kept many of the old skills alive during a fallow and difficult period for the craft.

The Exford smith's shop (ABOVE) could not present a more different face from the one at Merrow. It has clearly seen better days, for the thatch has worn wafer thin and will soon be letting in water. The rickety door is smothered with auctioneers' flyers for farm sales - the village forge had always been a meeting place for farmers where they could gossip and discuss the news of the day. The Exford smith is tightening the shoe of a hunter with pincers - this was an era when stag-hunting on the broad uplands of Exmoor was not a contentious issue in the country. The Exford smithy does not give much of an impression of progress, nor of successful adaptation to a very different future.

It would seem that not every village smith made the transition from farrier to motor mechanic.

The Monday Blues

THE HOUSEWIFE'S DREADED WEEKLY
LABOURS AT THE WASH TUB

Below:
Washing Day,
Shottery,
Warwickshire
c1890
S297548

TODAY, clothes washing involves the pressing of a button on a washing machine. In Victorian times this chore for the country housewife lasted for a whole day or more, and involved considerable stamina and muscle. Washing day was traditionally Mondays, for there was generally enough food left over from the Sunday meal to save another having to be cooked.

The choice of water was critical: where a stream was the source, the 'Instructions to the Laundry Maid' of 1815 suggested if the water was thick and muddy it was better left to stand for four days to clear. In hard water districts a piece of quicklime or soda lump might be added, and the mixture left to soften for a week. Heavily soiled clothes were left to soak in soda or lye, while more delicate garments were washed by hand in a tub of cold or luke-warm water. Rinsing was a vital part of the process - in towns there was rarely enough water for adequate rinsing, for the supply was restricted by law. In country areas soapy clothes were often rinsed in a stream.

Washing by hand was exhausting, and the invention of the peg dolly, which resembled a miniature three-legged stool with a long handle, was a considerable advance. It was twisted rapidly, and drove the linen through the wash water, spinning it out against the walls of the tub, causing the heavy dirt to collect out of the current.

Until the 1870s linen had been bleached in urine or hog's manure, and the more squeamish Victorian housewife of the 1890s must have welcomed the invention of the bleach with which we are familiar today. In villages, clothes were often laid out on the grass to be whitened by the sun.

A Quest for the Exotic

THE KITCHEN GARDEN AT PELL WALL HALL

Below:
The Kitchen Garden, Pell Wall Hall, near Market Drayton, Shropshire 1911
63372

THE KITCHEN GARDEN reached its zenith in the nineteenth century. The Victorians were ambitious and progressive by nature, believing that anything could be achieved if sufficient hard work, endeavour and investment were applied; the kitchen garden was the perfect place for this philosophy to be tried and tested. Also, the serious kitchen garden offered considerable scope for impressing your guests. As well as providing vegetables and fruit for the household all the year round, such a garden grew exotic blooms to decorate the rooms of the house - often these were chosen to complement the colours of the ladies' gowns - and, most important of all, it offered a range of exotic fruits and vegetables out of season to delight and amaze guests.

This, of course, involved forcing plants. John Ruskin called it a 'vile and gluttonous modern habit', but it was in character with the Victorian love of show and display. If a host were able to impress guests in spring with summer asparagus, rhubarb and artichokes, he would spare no expense in doing so. Cookery writers of the period very often condemned much of the forced

produce as being without colour, taste or flavour, but forcing went on all the same - the temptation to show off was irresistible.

Simply building a kitchen garden involved an immense investment. At Pell Wall Hall near Market Drayton, almost 300 yards of brick wall had to be built, and heating systems, cold frames and other equipment installed. Building the glass houses here was only possible because the government excise duty on glass had been removed.

The ceaseless quest for the exotic and unlikely generated a tremendous work load for the Pell Wall gardeners, who had to plan their work many months ahead. As autumn approached, fruit trees and bushes were encouraged out of their natural dormant state by syringing them with warm water. The boilers in the glass houses were stoked up with coals and the houses heated to protect the vulnerable plants against the cold winter nights.

The Pell Wall gardeners were kept busy by their employers the Munro Walkers (of the famous whisky distilling family), who were renowned for their lavish house parties. The stable block (ABOVE) would have been thronged throughout the year with grand motor cars. The forcing regime continued throughout the dark days of winter until, in the spring, the Munro Walkers surprised guests with their table displays of swags of grapes and fruit bowls heaped with apricots and plums. Their fuel bills must have been frightening.

The kitchen garden at Pell Wall was bordered by old walls of ruby red brick 12 feet high, and was 80 yards long and 60 wide. In the picture, taken in 1911, the head gardener and his assistants are

Above:
The Stable Block, Pell Wall Hall, near Market Drayton Shropshire 1911
63377

watering flowers which will be cut for the lavish and colourful house displays that the Munro Walkers loved so much. On the left are cordons of fruit trees, created from the painstaking training of branched espaliers. As well as being more productive and forming a pleasing fringe to the garden, these cordons were low enough to escape wind damage, and the Pell Wall gardeners could gather the crop without the use of ladders. On the far wall are what look like trained pear trees. In the glass houses the gardeners grew melons and other exotic fruits.

The house at Pell Wall, which was designed by John Soane, had a varied history. During this century it was both Catholic school and corset factory. More recently it was burned down and the shell taken into the ownership of the North Shropshire District Council. The shallow-roofed Garden House, now owned by Mr Peter Hill, is at the left of the picture, and from its door a broad central path bisected the garden from end to end.

The lovely old boat-shaped glass houses with their subtly-curved roofs almost all remain today, although some panes have tumbled and broken owing to rotted clips. Mr Hill intends to restore them to their former state.

Paradise Lost in the Lakes?

THE RELENTLESS INVASION OF WORDSWORTH'S BELOVED FELLS BY THE VICTORIAN WORKING MAN

WE ARE ALL WORRIED about the fate of our own favourite patch of rural Britain. Will they build a new estate in our favourite field, or a bypass through a beloved beauty spot? Such fears are not a new phenomenon, and were being loudly voiced by many throughout the nineteenth century.

The picture (BELOW RIGHT) shows the Bowness Ferry carrying a coach and four across Lake Windermere in 1896. The horses are steadied from the front by the ferryman, and the driver holds the reins in case the animals bolt: it is a chain ferry, and is drawn through the water by a steam-driven boat alongside, so a sudden hiss might startle the team. The well-to-do passengers silently contemplate the sublime fells made famous by the poet Wordsworth, enjoying the broad, breezy prospects. It is likely that this is a special excursion, and that the travellers are indulging themselves in a little nostalgia for the vanished days of the horse-drawn coach.

Things are not peaceful for long. A contemporary writer has recounted what happens next: there is laughter and singing, and the discordant sounds of a concertina; a brass band breaks into a popular tune on the quayside; then a 'nigger troupe' puts on a show on the

Below:
The Pleasure Steamer 'Teal' at Bowness, Cumbria 1896
38795

Right:
The Ferry Boat, Bowness 1896
38800

landing stage. The startled passengers on the coach quickly avert their eyes as a steamer carrying trippers, who have arrived from the dark satanic mills of Lancashire, ties up. It is, said the critic, 'perfect pandemonium'. The steamer 'Teal' (OPPOSITE PAGE, BELOW) is called a 'pleasure' boat, but it is hard to imagine what pleasure there can be packed tight like sardines with two hundred and fifty other passengers. The steamer is sitting perilously low in the water.

Such scenes were common during the summer in the normally peaceful Lakes, and had been for some years. In a letter to the builders of the Kendal and Windermere railway, Wordsworth had

Left:
The Lake District beloved of Wordsworth
c1870
18663

Below:
**The Ferry Boat,
Bowness 1896**
38802

Bottom:
**Waterhead,
Windermere,
Cumbria 1912**
64319

written passionately: 'Is there no nook of English ground secure from rash assault?'

The 'culprits' were in many cases the mill owners, sending their workers on daytrips to break the monotony of the factory slog. Wordsworth writes to the *Morning Post* that the 'advance of the ten thousand' will do no one any good. He believes that appreciation of the Lakes is a 'cultivated taste ... surely that good is not to be obtained by transferring at once uneducated persons in large bodies to particular spots? ...' He goes further, suggesting that the morals of the local rural population would be surely compromised by the inevitable 'wrestling matches, horse and boat races without number, and pot-houses and beer shops' that would proliferate. The Sabbath day in the towns of Bowness and Ambleside would be 'subject to much additional desecration'.

It is hard to sympathise with Wordsworth's uncompromising elitism, but one only has to read 'The Prelude' to understand what the lakes and fells of this unique region of Britain meant to him. The photograph (PREVIOUS PAGE, TOP) of the hoary old fellow standing solitary at a field gate presents an image of the Lakeland scenery that the poet was so passionately keen to preserve. For Wordsworth, the Lakes were a place for silent contemplation, a shrine for poetic thought and solitary meditation on mankind and nature.

Wordsworth's eloquent plea did not win the day. The railways spread their tentacles, and the steamers at the

Windermere quayside proliferated. The trippers on the 'Teal' have had a long day's journey: from Blackburn, Burnley and Preston, they have sailed across Morecambe Bay, gone by rail to Lake Side, then by steamer to Ambleside for tea; finally a coach has carried them to Coniston, and then a steamer will take them back to Fleetwood and the mills. The Lakes must have seemed a paradise to them, a world far removed from their everyday lives. Every Victorian was a deep romantic at heart, and the Lakes with their wild and majestic scenery had an immense appeal, especially in that they could be reached in a day's journey by rail, coach and steamer. Lake Windermere, the most popular destination, possessed an incomparable richness of islands and wooded shores.

Meanwhile, our coach has dropped off its passengers at the new hotels that have sprung up along the lake side. Some have come to try out the remedial bathing at the popular Windermere Hydropathic Hotel at Bowness: from being a tiny remote village, Bowness now had forty-three boarding-houses catering for the middle classes. Others have journeyed on to Ambleside to stay at the Queen's Hotel (ABOVE), where they can enjoy further excursions to Keswick and Coniston. Here they are obliged to jostle with further crowds of trippers from the industrial north, who have just arrived from Waterhead (OPPOSITE PAGE, BELOW). Others wait patiently to board Higgs' coaches bound for Windermere.

Above:
Market Place, Ambleside, Cumbria 1912
64302

Intrepid Pathfinders at Saffron Walden

AN EXQUISITE RECONSTRUCTED VICTORIAN MAZE

THEY HAVE made it! The two weary explorers rest after battling their way to the centre of the maze at Saffron Walden in Essex. The head gardener looks on with a wicked grin - he has already charged them 6d to get into the maze. If he was feeling just a little bit unscrupulous he could charge them another 6d to get out.

The Frith photographer, perched on a central iron viewing platform, could taunt them as they floundered, stumbling from dead end to dead end. It was all very easy up on top with a commanding panoramic view: 'Keep following the left-hand hedge in and out of every turn'.

This superb Victorian yew hedge maze was laid out and planted in the Italianate style by Francis Gibson in the 1840s as part of the delightful Bridge End Gardens. It is thought that its designer was William Andrews Nesfield, renowned for laying out an Italianate style maze for the Great Exhibition in 1851.

The two thousand feet of narrow, close-clipped paths were decorated with a Chinese pavilion, much ornate statuary and columns, and seats where you could rest or squabble about the route with your partner.

Records show that by 1905 the maze was open to the public, and it continued to tax visitors' patience and endurance until the late 1940s.

The old yew hedges were trimmed regularly for years. Then, after a century of constant care they began to be neglected and allowed to bolt, and the maze deteriorated.By 1983 it had fallen into disrepair and was no more than an overgrown spinney. Very little of the maze structure was still discernible.

Then Uttlesford District Council resolved to take on the daunting task of reconstruction. During 1984 the site was cleared and excavated by Tony Collins and John Bosworth. A number of oyster shells and Victorian wine bottles were found, bearing testimony to the fact that when visitors did get stuck they resolved to enjoy the experience.

Using triangulation, the original maze pattern was re-established and the paths marked out with liquid lime. They were then dug out and dressed with shingle. Well over a thousand three-year old yews (*Taxus Baccata*) were planted at 525mm intervals, and the iron gates restored.

In 1991, the restored maze was officially reopened by Anthony Fry, great grandson of Francis Gibson, the maze's Victorian founder.

A Ruin with a View

THE AMATEUR PAINTER AT BOLTON ABBEY

AMONGST a picturesque setting of meadows and woodland, a young woman watches her husband painting a watercolour at Bolton Abbey in Yorkshire.

In the background are the romantic ruins of the Augustinian priory and, to the right, the tumbling waters of the River Wharfe.

Landseer and Turner are just two of the many painters who have been drawn to the sublime scenery around the abbey. Photographers, too, have found it irresistible - Francis Frith exposed fifty glass plates here during a single visit. Bolton Abbey is rich in prospects for the artistic eye: there are the stepping stones across the river, the deep green hanging woods, the lively bubbling waters, and the ancient stones of the ruined 14th-century chancel.

Many young Victorian women employed drawing masters, but it is unlikely that the artist in the picture is teaching this young woman to paint: she has her hand on his shoulder, an unthinkable thing to do in public unless they were married.

Professional artists often complained bitterly about the numbers of amateurs who congregated with their drawing masters at popular beauty spots. On many summer weekends they found it almost impossible to get near the scene they wished to paint because of tutors 'teaching the unteachable misses'.

Below:
Bolton Abbey, Yorkshire 1886
18510

With Featheries and Clubbis

Below:
**The Links,
Criccieth, Gwynedd**
1913 65789

Bottom:
**The Golf Links,
Mullion, Cornwall**
1911 64023

MODERN professional golfers make driving, chipping and putting look supremely simple, for they benefit from the latest technology: an aerodynamic ball, and clubs that are well balanced and manufactured from a precise blend

HOW A DAY OUT ON THE LINKS BECAME A FAVOURITE PASTIME OF ASPIRING VICTORIANS

of metals. Yet golfers did not always enjoy these advantages. How well might today's professionals perform with a soft 'featherie', the golf ball that was used until 1850? Made from boiled feathers, it was about as aerodynamic as a haggis. Early Victorian golf clubs were hardly more effective, and were spoken of as 'rude and clumsy bludgeons'. The greens, too, were very different from the silken variety enjoyed by even the most ordinary amateur today: holes were often hacked out with a pen knife, with the marker flag no more than a feather, and the only green keepers were the rabbits.

Before the nineteenth century you could hardly have played at all outside Scotland. King James IV, with his royal 'golf clubbis and ballis', encouraged the sport, and Scots had enjoyed their national game on breezy coastal links like St Andrews since 1700. It was not until the 1860s that golf came to England; the first club to be founded was the North Devon at Westward Ho.

The sport quickly caught the public imagination in England and Wales. The handicapping system was a highly effective leveller, allowing players of any standard to compete. It is hardly surprising that golf grew in popularity with the emerging commercial middle classes, for courses could normally be found within easy reach of the towns and cities where they lived and worked.

Above:
**The Clubhouse,
Hindhead
Golf Club,
Surrey 1907**
57883

The more traditional gentlemen's pursuits of hunting, shooting and fishing required considerably greater leisure time than most working people could afford. Being 'in a meeting' on the links became a popular form of office work on hot summer afternoons.

At Harlech (OPPOSITE PAGE), golfers could enjoy the picturesque prospects of the castle and headland as they walked between holes, and at Mullion (PREVIOUS PAGE), they could hear the thundering of the waves on the rocks below while enjoying the sea breezes. Golfing dress - the ubiquitous Norfolk jacket and breeches - was refreshingly informal in a society which prided itself on its propriety.

As one might guess, life was not so simple for the Victorian woman golfer. She had to balance a straw boater on her head, while sweltering under the weight of ankle-length tweed skirts and thick boots. She could only use a putter, for it was thought unseemly for a woman to raise a club above shoulder level. The Ladies' Golf Union was founded in 1893.

The photograph of Hindhead Golf Club (ABOVE) was taken in 1907, just three years after the club had been founded. Members believe that the golfer on the left is the author Conan Doyle: the author of the famous Sherlock Holmes stories lived locally and was President of the club from 1905 to 1907.

Golf clubs were usually constructed in exposed, open countryside, and there were often bitter local disputes concerning the impact of clubhouse buildings on the landscape. Planning permission was unheard of in those days; but nevertheless, the founding members at Hindhead were keen to avoid any confrontations. The intended site was set in very beautiful countryside close to the picturesque Devil's Punch Bowl. In 1885 a local guidebook by a Mr Morris had praised the region's 'unspoilt, primitive rusticity'. A few years later in 1903, he was noting some worrying developments, and shuddering at a certain glaring red brick house that was peeping over the Punch Bowl rim: 'There amid perky larches and pine, And over the sullen purple moor, Look at it pricking a cockney ear'.

The founders of Hindhead Golf Club steered their architect firmly away from 'glaring' red brick and chose a more sober sand-coloured stucco. The final clubhouse was a curious confection, and has been described in the club's official history as 'a pair of lop-sided gable-ended Dutch barns on top of a pillared verandah with a narrow balcony above set between two octagonal towers surmounted by squat steeples'. The Frith picture shows only a single tower - a mirror-image of the building in the picture was added in 1909. A clubhouse in the early 1900s involved more than just a simple changing room and bar: there had to be servants' quarters, a scullery, larder, boiler room, coal and wood stores, and a separate room for 'boots and irons'. One alteration to the original design that was suggested was to raise the height of the kitchen windows so that servants could not peer at members taking refreshments on the verandah outside. The clubhouse at Hindhead was an immediate success with local golfers, and membership grew rapidly after its official opening in 1906.

Criccieth Golf Club, established in 1905, is a parkland course set high above Cardigan Bay. The landscape in the 1913 photograph (SEE FIRST PAGE OF CHAPTER) gives the appearance of great antiquity, with low stone walls and irregularly shaped fields where sheep graze. Here, the club professional, Mr Owens, is offering instruction at the first hole. Lloyd George was once President of the Club.

Below:
The Castle
and Golf Links,
Harlech,
Gwynedd 1908
60251

Caverns Measureless to Man

THE STORY OF THE DISCOVERY OF THE WORLD-FAMOUS
COX'S CAVE IN CHEDDAR GORGE

OLD SALLY SPENCER walks with her stick down the steep lane into Cheddar in 1908 (MAIN PICTURE).

In the background are the spectacular contours of Lion Rock. William Parsons, her great-great-grandson, recalls how Sally Spencer made her living by collecting and selling to visitors fragments of spar chipped from the sides of the Gorge. The hills above the village are rich in flowers that peep out from rock fissures into the sunlight, and Sally also found a ready market for the local Cheddar pinks. Her brother, 'Roper' Parsons, was a local rope-maker, and no doubt his ropes averted disaster more than once in the depths of Cox's caves.

Cox's cavern has been called 'the most exquisite in the world', but was only discovered by accident. In 1837 Edward Cox, proprietor of the Cliff Hotel, was cutting back into the rockface across the lane to make more space for his guests' carts and carriages. Workmen were very surprised when they broke through into a hole that was soon to

Below:
Cox's Cave,
Cheddar,
Somerset,
date unknown
C71037

become one of the great wonders of the natural world.

Edward Cox instructed them to dig down into the darkness. Soon he was announcing wonders that were not to be missed: a Hindoo Temple, a Marble Curtain and beautiful mirror-like pools, which reflected the shapes of stalactites in the water below. Cox's cavern swiftly became world-famous: one advertisement proclaimed how 'all the 600 chief caves in the world have been visited by Monsieur Martel. He gives the palm to Cox's stalactite cavern'.

Edward Cox was not alone in making money out of Cheddar curiosities: local village lads were hacking off as many stalactites as they could to sell to keen collectors. Some even used shotguns to bring down stalactites that hung high up in the cave roofs.

Later Frith views show charabancs queueing to drop off eager passengers. Harry Savory, the famous caver, visited Cox's cavern in 1910 and reported on the new network of paths, which had been widened for large parties. He lamented the breaking off of stalactites by careless workmen - many broken pieces had been carelessly plastered

Below:
Sally Spencer at Glen Middle Mill, Cheddar 1908 60144

back into place in the hope that no-one would notice.

By Sally Spencer's time Cheddar had spawned souvenir shops, cafes and yet more hotels to cater for visitors. She must have been grateful to the caves for providing her with a regular income.

Because of vandalism down the years, early photographs of the cave interiors show distinct differences from those taken today. Francis Frith was one of the very first photographers to brave the depths.

By 1866 he was announcing a series of eighteen spectacular prints. Taking them would have been fraught with difficulties: photographic emulsions were painfully slow at that time, and only gas and oil flares would have been available to light the enormous black voids. Frith must have shown creditable courage and patience as he stood in the silent depths of the cave in the flickering lamp-light, and while he clambered up and down a long, quivering ladder hauling his heavy brass camera.

Below:
**Entrance to Pass,
Cheddar 1908**
60134

Efficacious in Every Way

MALVERN'S PURE WATER AND SOME SPARTAN CELEBRITY CURES

DOWN THE centuries people have retained a firm and unshakeable belief in the curative and beneficial properties of natural spring waters. Bubbling from ancient rocks, these mineral waters have seemed to many to be imbued with a holy or supernatural force.

At spas like Bath and Harrogate the mineral waters were said to have a slightly unpleasant taste on the palate owing to their organic content. At Malvern the water was particularly pure. Dr John Wall claimed that it would 'pass through the vessels of the body' better than other spring waters. Malvern water was advertised as 'a table water of the highest class. Remarkably pure ... it has long been celebrated for its curative properties against rheumatism, gout, scrofula and affections of the liver and kidneys. Its methodical use is calculated to prevent the formation of morbid concretions and deposits'.

Holy Well, J. H. Cuff's Mineral Water

Below:
**Great Malvern,
Worcestershire**
c1874
7071b

factory (RIGHT), sits at the foot of the imposing Malvern hills. It houses an ancient spring that trickles out of the bare granite, and has been in use since medieval times. In 1654 John Evelyn reported how it was said 'to heale many infirmities, such as king's evil, leaprosie, sore eyes etc'. Most 'holy' wells had none of the direct associations with saints enjoyed by wells in the Celtic west. Dorothy Hartley, in 'Water in England', explains how custodians of ancient springs often found it both convenient and diplomatic to make a saint's goodness responsible for the cure, and a patient's crimes responsible for the disease. Prayers invariably accompanied the taking of the waters, and it is not surprising that many springs and wells grew to become places of pilgrimage.

The water from Holy Well was renowned in particular for its special efficacy in treating eye problems. Bottling began as early as 1622 - a contemporary song records that a thousand bottles were shipped weekly to London, Berwick and Kent. By 1747 there were houses and apartments here for visitors, and business continued to be brisk.

The cottage ornée-style factory in the photograph was built in 1843 at a cost of £400 - note its somewhat eccentric battlemented detailing and imposing Norman-style doorway. In 1850 the famous bottlers Schweppes sub-leased the supply, and it was not until 1895 that J. H. Cuff took over the business. The bottling plant was run successfully for many years, but by the 1950s the building had fallen into dilapidation. In the 1970s John Parkes bought it and set about a thorough restoration. Bottling began again in earnest - one regular client was said to be Buckingham Palace - and only stopped again in 1990. The fate of the building and of the old spring it houses is now uncertain.

The wells around the town of Malvern attracted visitors throughout the Victorian period, and it gained a reputation as an important spa town. Soon the streets were filled with bath-chairs, containing pale men and women wrapped in shawls. Doctors Wilson and Gully set up a hydropathic establishment in the town with a course of treatment based on the spartan Czechoslovak method.

Patients took cold baths, spent hours bandaged in wringing wet sheets, suffered icy douches, and stood naked under fierce cascades of freezing cold water. Douches were considered beneficial for painful joints and for the circulation. The pounding of the falling water and its icy coldness restored the circulation, and keeping the affected joint wrapped in flannel afterwards would bring back mobility. These curious treatments can be compared to today's alternative health therapies. Fashionable society and many 19th-century celebrities and worthies, including Gladstone, Macaulay, Dickens and Carlyle - even Florence Nightingale - came to Malvern to take the cure.

Right:
Holy Well,
Malvern Wells,
Worcestershire 1904
51153

Please – No Volleying

HOW GOOD BEHAVIOUR ON COURT COULD HELP A YOUNG WOMAN MAKE HER WAY IN VICTORIAN SOCIETY

THE PICTURE on the opposite page shows a tennis tournament at Moffat in Scotland in 1892. A mixed doubles match is under way. The ladies, as in all Victorian sports, are at a considerable disadvantage with their long, billowing dresses and broad-brimmed hats.

Before tennis became popular only the well-to-do young woman could enjoy herself in mixed-sex sports, by following the traditional upper-class recreations like hunting and riding. Women from the rising commercial classes were at a distinct disadvantage. Tennis, however, offered them a unique opportunity to discover new circles of friends, as well as meet suitable young men in sedate doubles matches. By Edwardian times tennis was a must at garden parties.

Tactics would have favoured today's base-line players: it was considered very bad form to dash to the net and volley or smash. Lobbing was unheard-of, and the ball was to be patted gently back and forth.

Ladies were allowed to serve under-arm: if they had made any attempt at over-arm serving they would have knocked off their hats. The tennis authorities had suggested that the ball should be allowed to bounce twice to give the ladies time to get about the court, but the idea was rejected.

Opposite page:
A Mixed Doubles Tennis Match, Moffat, Dumfries and Galloway 1892
M113003

Below:
Tennis Courts, The Gardens, Buxton, Derbyshire 1886
18659

An Unhurried Tradition Down on the Farm

THE OLD-STYLE COUNTRY FARMYARD

Left:
Ovey's Farm,
Cookham,
Berkshire 1914
67019

IT WOULD BE almost impossible to find a farm like Ovey's anywhere today. It is a scene of ramshackle but benign chaos. Hens scratch in the grass and shelter from the sun in the shadow of the rough wooden feeders, which have been endlessly repatched with odd lengths of wood. Even the tall chimney of the farmhouse is slumped soporifically against the gable end. The horse, still in the traces, tunnels deep into its nosebag. The tumbril is of a traditional design, artfully hinged with an iron pin, so it can be tipped to unload manure in yard or fields. The farmer, George Hatch, stands in his waistcoat in silent contemplation.

Ovey's was never a significant farm, and its holding was modest. The house itself has ancient origins: English Heritage discovered evidence of medieval timber-framing and traces of a Saxon screened hall here. The barn on the right, with its high loft door for storing hay delivered by an elevator, was demolished in 1969.

Ovey's ceased to be a working farm in the early 1920s. Many small farms that had been passed down the generations, and which had endured even the most severe of the agricultural depressions of 1880s and 1890s, failed to adapt to changing practices and fashions.

All Is Safely Gathered In

HOW HORSE-DRAWN MACHINES
HASTENED THE HARVEST

WE TEND to think that period sepia photographs of farming scenes portray a countryside that was unchanging and eternal - the farmers in smocks, field workers scything by hand or ploughing a single furrow with horses. Yet from the late Victorian period, when most of the Frith images were taken, the fields were an arena in which fundamental changes were taking place. Brand new inventions, implements and machinery were displacing the manual labourer in

Above:
**Mowing at
Fittleworth,
Sussex c1940**
F29047

Right:
**Haymaking at
Hawes,
Yorkshire 1924**
75754

the fields and an entire era was nearing its end.

In the photograph of Fittleworth (OPPOSITE PAGE, TOP) the horses have taken a break to shake off the flies and to catch their breath in the shade of the hedge. They have been mowing the headlands. The grass at their feet is thick with flower heads, not a sight with which we would be very familiar today, for our meadows are sprayed to keep unwanted plants out. The horses sniff the air - they have an acute sense of smell, and the old farmers believed that the scent of flowers and grasses had a soothing effect on them.

With the coming of summer it was time for haymaking. The fresh green grass was cut in late June and stored in ricks for the cattle to feed on during the months of winter. Haymaking old-style

Above:
The Horse Rake at Work, Cheam, Surrey 1925
77074

could take three or four days, and the fields around every village were busy with workers labouring with scythe, rake and pitchfork.

In the 1924 photograph of haymaking at Hawes in the Yorkshire Dales (LEFT), much of the fieldwork is clearly still being carried out by hand. The hay has been cut, then turned and fluffed up so the wind and sun could gently dry it. The horse draws a sledge which will be heaped with the sweet-smelling hay. Farmers are resourceful at adapting their machinery to local conditions: on these high, steep slopes wheels would have dug into the soft grass, and a sledge was the perfect solution.

The new machines hastened the process considerably, but robbed hay-making of much of its romance and sense of community. In June the grass would be cut with a horse-drawn mower (see the view of Fittleworth). The sun was allowed to carry out its job of drying, and then the grass was tossed and fluffed with a machine tedder to break up the wisps and to air them. Then came the horse-rake (ABOVE RIGHT),

Above:
A Self-Binder at Work, Lustleigh, Devon 1920
69626

which raked the dried grass into tidy lines. It was hauled across the field behind the horse and drew the scattered heaps of grass into its curved hollow rake where it remained trapped. From time to time the driver would lift the rake by means of a lever, so freeing the hay which lay in curving rows awaiting the waggons, which can be seen in the background. Carters forked the golden hay onto the waggons until they were close to toppling, then drove them back to the farm ready for the rick builders.

Rick building was a skilled job - some conical-topped ricks are shown at West Lulworth in 1904 (OPPOSITE PAGE, TOP). Most farms had a special field close to the farmhouse where the ricks were built, for it was important to keep a wary eye on them. If the hay was a little too wet when it had been carried from the field it might sweat in the rick and grow so hot that it could burst into flames. Storms, too, caused damage, dragging off the simple thatch top, allowing rain to penetrate and ruin the hay.

During August the wheat, barley and oats were cut and gathered. In 1899 the writer and farmer Rider Haggard reported that he had set his new reaper to work on a field of oats. 'It is a beautiful thing to see it work, for it cuts wonderfully clean, the arms sweeping the bundles of corn from the platform in sheaves, ready for the binder.' But as with all machines the smooth ride did not last for long: the machine had an irritating tendency to jam when the driver was turning it at the headlands. Rider Haggard used two horses for the task and changed them over at noon, for he believed that half a day's work pulling a reaper was quite enough for two animals. He reports, too, a terrible accident involving a reaper: the horse team bolted, and in trying to stop them their owner was thrown to the ground. He was so cut about by the knives under the machine that he died.

The beautiful view of Lustleigh (OPPOSITE PAGE, LEFT) shows a reaping scene with a self-binder. This device cut the oats, drew them into sheaves and tied them. Self-binders are still used today for binding wheat sheaves for thatchers - modern combines tend to crush the stems, destroying their water-proof properties and durability.

Right:
Ricks at West Lulworth, Dorset 1904
52709

Below:
Loading the Waggons, Garboldisham, Norfolk c1940
G188029

Winter Gold in the Scillies

IN ABOUT 1870 William Trevillick packed a few home-grown Scilly White narcissi in his Aunt Ellen's hatbox and sent them over the Channel to Covent Garden market. They made 7/6. Delighted and surprised - for there was little public demand for cut flowers at the time - he sent some more. From this unlikely beginning grew the world-famous flower industry that has caused the Scillies to be called the Paradise Islands and the Lotus Isles.

THE BIRTH OF THE FAMOUS SPRING FLOWER INDUSTRY

It was a fortunate development, for in the early Victorian years the Scillonians were close to starvation. They had never taken to fishing, and even their half-hearted attempts at smuggling proved unsuccessful. The unique balmy climate of the Isles made flower growing economically viable, for there were few

days when the sun did not show itself, and gales were uncommon visitants.

While the rest of Victorian Britain was shivering in front of a smoky fire, the Scillonians were enjoying a blaze of colour. In the dead months of winter the fields around St Mary's were aflame with narcissi and daffodils, including dainty Scilly Whites, paper whites and the rich soleil d'or. A little later, in early spring, came the irises, tulips, stocks and violets. The Scillonians worked hard for their harvest, and since Trevillick's time they managed to turn his humble experiment into a staple industry. By 1886, they were growing and selling 160 varieties of narcissus. A season's export might amount to almost five million bunches.

This forcing of flowers was a very worrying business to be in: despite the beneficial climate, growers were at the mercy of the weather, and endlessly searched the winter skies for signs of the freezing salt-laden winds which threatened disaster to the crop. A contemporary writer spoke of the 'biting blast' which could 'hurtle around sunny Scilly in mad bewilderment', causing disfiguring and 'fatal taint' to the blooms. There was endless work to be done: the fields had to be ploughed with horses to make safe beds for the bulbs, which were planted between June and October, and then there were three years of constant hoeing and weeding before a crop could be taken.

In spring, every available man, woman and child devoted themselves to the flower harvest, plucking, bunching and packing the half-opened blooms. Packets waited at the quay to be loaded to the gunwales with boxes of flowers. Sometimes, when the market was a little depressed, it was not uncommon to see entire fields of delicate flowers left drooping to die because 'they won't pay to pick'.

It was traditional for the men to work in the fields picking the flowers in bud and loading them into wicker baskets. Meanwhile, behind the closed doors of a hundred cottages, in an atmosphere so overpowering with the scent of flowers that a mainlander might faint, women and children worked at selecting and discarding, bunching, tying and packing; there were twelve blooms to a bunch, twenty-four bunches to a box. Expert tiers could manage a hundred bunches in an hour. It was vital to keep 'lily rash' at bay - this was caused by flower sap.

The islanders' enterprise and efforts carried them out of their poverty and uncertainty, so that flower culture became the staple industry of the Isles.

Below:
The Tying House,
Scilly Isles 1894
33726

Through the Dappled Green Aisles

HOPS AND HOPPING IN THE GARDEN OF ENGLAND

AT GOUDHURST and Paddock Wood, and in many other villages throughout the south-eastern county of Kent, are the great gardens and oast-houses devoted to the growing and processing of the hop. Introduced to England from Flanders in the 1600s, this ancient plant, well known to the Romans, is cultivated for its very special catkins, which bring to beer its unique aromatic bitter taste.

A mature hop-garden in late summer is an exquisite sight, with bines trained over numberless rows of wires and lofty poles, called hop alleys, forming vistas of green foliage, gilded with garlands of golden hops. However, this glorious sight is not won easily by either farmer or picker.

Hops demand warmth and shelter to prosper, and much skilled cultivation in their long growing season - it takes three years for them to mature. At Goudhurst during the days of traditional cultivation (LEFT), there was laborious and painstaking work to be carried out during every single season: in winter the old bines had to be cleared away and burned, the land ploughed, and the poles and wires on which the hops were suspended had to be fully refurbished. Throughout each growing season, the hop plants required continual spraying with nicotine or quassia to fight the swarms of insect pests that preyed on them - see the picture of washing in a Tonbridge hop-garden (OPPOSITE PAGE, CENTRE). Varieties were selected by the grower for their hardiness, the size of the catkins, and resistance to disease and pests. Some of the most popular and widely-grown varieties were the Bramling, Fuggle's and Golding's, all named after the growers who bred them.

Towards the end of the summer of their third year, the ripening fruits began to swell and to acquire a scent. In the final stage of cultivation the 'stilt-men' appeared. On lofty stilts eighteen feet high, they picked a path between the rows, tying the topmost bines to the tallest strings to keep the ripening plants aloft. Once the plump cones were firm and crisp in the hand it was time for the pickers to enter the fray.

Many hundreds were employed by Kent growers. At hop harvest armies of the London poor travelled out by train and waggon to enjoy a few weeks of healthy open-air labour. It must have seemed like paradise, with the sun streaming down and with the fresh country smells and greenery. In the

Previous Page:
In the Hop-Field, Goudhurst, Kent 1904
52570

Below:
In the Hop-Field, Goudhurst, Kent 1904
52571d

photograph of Goudhurst (OPPOSITE PAGE) the pickers pose for the Frith photographer in the dappled shade. Men, women and children laboured from dawn to dusk in the dusty hop fields, sweltering in the sultry heat. The work was onerous and repetitive, but it not only provided them with a welcome income, it renewed their bodies and spirits, so they returned home to their cramped tenements and slum streets considerably restored. No matter that the rain sometimes fell pitiless and unrelenting, or that their clothes were scratched and torn and their boot soles worn paper-thin on the rough ground, they never failed to return the next year for more 'opping. It seems likely that the pickers in the photograph have arrived only recently, for the pinafore dresses of the little girls are bright white. They would not have stayed in this pristine state for very long.

This ragged army had to work fast, for the hops needed to be picked as soon as they were ripe. It was one man's task to cut the supporting strings that held the hops aloft with a bill-hook, causing the plants to collapse and fall haphazardly down on the heads of the assembled hop-pickers below. Straight away, the bines were stripped of their harvest by a thousand nimble fingers. The pickers worked in small groups, each having a bin to fill with hops. The bin was in the form of a large sack spread out over a rough wooden frame, which could be moved gradually across the field as the work progressed. Bushellers employed by the grower made their rounds several times a day, collecting and measuring the hops. They offloaded them into pokes, which were loose sacks holding up to ten bushels.

Towards the day's end the call went up over the fields, 'Pull no more poles!' and the brigades of pickers trooped off to kindle fires, prepare their evening meal, and to enjoy a well-earned rest. It was a time of joy and comradeship, despite the gruelling work under the hot sun. The humour was boisterous and a little too much beer could be drunk by some, but in general the atmosphere was good-hearted, and enjoyed by everyone.

Above:
Washing the Hops, Tonbridge, Kent 1890
T1015009

Right:
Measuring the Hops, Paddock Wood, Kent c1940
P220009

A Slow Plod from Prehistory

THE OX AS A DRAUGHT ANIMAL ON A COTSWOLD FARM

THE OX has been a beast of burden since prehistory. It was used in the medieval village to plough the long, curving strips of land that were characteristic of the open field system, but was gradually replaced by horses, which although not as strong, were swifter over light land.

However, in the first years of the 18th century, oxen were reintroduced as draught animals on many Cotswold farms, including Lord Bathurst's estate at Cirencester Park. New genetic strains were bred, and contemporary paintings show mammoth prize beasts with dwarfish legs that look as if they could never ever support the weight of muscle and flesh.

New ploughs were developed in the latter years of the 19th century that were specifically suited to the horse, and once again the ox was displaced. Yet Lord Bathurst, probably out of a sense of tradition, retained his team right up until the 1940s, showing them off at exhibitions and county shows.

The ox may have a slow, plodding gait but he is not lacking in intelligence. Oxen are said to have a very strong homing instinct, and are capable of travelling hundreds of miles back to the place where they were bred.

The ox had two distinct advantages over the horse: he could eat rougher food and was therefore cheaper to keep, and he could be fattened up and sold at market, once he had been worked for a few years.

Below:
Oxen at Lord Bathurst's Estate, Cirencester Park, Gloucestershire 1898
40986

Miss Clapp's Beloved Cleeve

A SOMERSET CISTERCIAN ABBEY'S FALL AND RESURRECTION

Right:
The Gatehouse,
Cleeve Abbey,
Somerset 1890
27524

Below:
The Abbot's
House,
Cleeve Abbey,
Somerset 1919
69284

'IS NOT this place haunted?' asked a visitor. 'Only by the good,' replied Cleeva Clapp, who spent almost all her life at this ancient Somerset Cistercian abbey in the first part of this century.

Cleeve is indeed atmospheric: many of its buildings are still so complete that the centuries quickly fall away, and you feel the presence of the white-habited, silent monks who paced its cloisters five hundred years ago.

Life was hard for them. They must have been chilled to the bone much of the time, kneeling at prayer on the lime-ash floors and labouring in the muddy fields. Only a single fire was allowed in the abbey - in the drying-room, where sheepskins were dried and the monks gathered to warm themselves. They slept on straw mattresses on the cold, hard floor of the communal dorter (OVERLEAF, TOP), a long first-floor chamber. (In the 15th century, luckier brethren enjoyed beds in cubicles). They rose soon after midnight to creep along the dark dorter, carrying a lamp down the night stairs to matins.

Henry VIII destroyed Cleeve's abbey church at the Dissolution. Later, one of the buildings was converted into a farmhouse, part of the cloisters into a cottage, and the central garden into a farmyard. Manure steamed in heaps in the chapter house, and a stone wall across the centre of the court kept the pigs and sheep apart. In the 1870s the beautiful upstairs refectory was filled

Below:
**The Refectory
and Dorter,
Cleeve Abbey**
c1875 5988

Bottom:
**The Refectory,
Cleeve Abbey**
c1885 7931

with barrels, hurdles and sheaves; in the medieval wall-painting above them, the fading Christ on the cross stared down at this perpetual harvest tribute (OPPOSITE PAGE).

In 1875, the Luttrells of Dunster Castle, who owned Cleeve Abbey, began a programme of restoration. Much of the work was recorded in a sequence of fine photographic studies by Francis Frith. The Luttrells eventually leased the abbey to the local policeman, Constable Clapp. The farmhouse was converted into three cottages, and Constable Clapp's daughter, Cleeva - named after the abbey - lived in one of them.

She had a passion for this ancient ruin that lasted throughout her life, opening it up to the public and giving guided tours. The plot of ground outside the refectory was turned into a market garden, where Captain Angelo, who lived in the third of the cottages, sold his giant Himalayan tomatoes to abbey visitors. Cleeva Clapp sold cream teas and enthused to everyone, deeply in love with her building. At this time, Cleeve had a comforting domestic look, with washing on the line and vegetables sprouting at every corner: the picture of the refectory (BOTTOM) shows Cleeva Clapp's fine display of vegetables.

In 1876, a fine medieval tiled pavement was discovered here under the soil, the floor of the original refectory.

The buildings in Cleeva Clapp's era would have seemed very different to the monks. In their time, the walls were plastered inside and out, and must have dazzled in the sunlight. The cloisters extended all the way round, and the monks would sit studying in the shade, or looking out at the lay brothers who were tending the central herb garden. In the 19th century wooden panelling was inserted into the tracery to form a makeshift farmworker's cottage.

When the Ministry of Works took over the building in the 1950s, they began a long and arduous restoration programme to secure the structure. Now English Heritage is conserving Cleeve's ancient stones, returning the abbey from a farm to a national monument.

Above:
The Refectory
and Faded Wall
Painting of Christ,
Cleeve Abbey
1913
65348

A Hillside Enigma

A PERPLEXING STONE CIRCLE

THIS EXTENSIVE circle of stones above the town of Pontypridd is not as ancient as it may appear. It was conceived and built in 1850 by a local antiquary Evan Davis, for his initiation as Arch Druid of the revived National Eisteddfod. The two fine concentric circles enclose the Rocking Stone, which is a genuine glacial erratic.

The Eisteddfod has ancient origins going back to the 12th century, but a national event had not been held since the Elizabethan era. Then in the 1790s the old ceremony of the National Eisteddfod was revived. Sixty years later, Evan Davis, fired with enthusiasm by the antiquarian William Stukeley and his theories about Druidism, built this circle on the hill above Pontypridd, based on the Avebury configuration.

The circle was used for ceremonial processions and Bardic ritual three or four times a year up until the 1920s. Evan Davis set into motion a custom of constructing a new stone circle for each successive National Eisteddfod, and examples can be found in many Welsh locations, including Cardiff and Mountain Ash. In the foreground of the picture are the sacred Bardic signs, carved in stone and wood.

Below:
Evan Davis's
Stone Circle,
Pontypridd,
Mid Glamorgan
1899
43622

A Romantick, Holy Place

THE OLD CHURCH OF ST BONIFACE AT BONCHURCH

Right:
The Church of
St Boniface,
Bonchurch, Isle of
Wight c1880
8781

Below:
St Boniface
Church Porch
c1880
8159

DURING the early Victorian era there was scant respect for old churches, and the fabric of many was allowed to deteriorate. The walls were damp, ivy invaded the mortar and prised apart the stones, and slates fell from the roofs during storms, leaving the rafters exposed to the skies. The churchyard paths were often impassable because of the invading ranks of stiff nettles, and many old neglected headstones and monuments slumped and toppled.

In some unlucky villages 'restorers' were called in. Their remedies were invariably worse than the disease they had come to treat: they removed the patina of age, ripped up old stone floors and replaced them with brightly-coloured industrial tiles, demolished arcades to raise roofs or to create further aisles, and installed stained glass bought from a jobber's pattern book. They saved their direst deeds for the chancel, for the fashion was for garish decoration, and the plain old stones were not considered holy enough.

Bonchurch on the Isle of Wight is a strikingly picturesque village between the sea and a steep down smothered with deep green trees. Dickens stayed close by at Winterbourne in 1849 and praised the landscape fulsomely: 'There are views which are only equalled on the Genoese shore ... the variety of walks is extraordinary'. From the early 19th century Bonchurch was highly fashionable with well-to-do visitors, and it expanded quickly, with villas marching relentlessly over the down.

Above:
The Churchyard,
St Boniface
Church,
Bonchurch,
Isle of Wight
c1890
26153

The ancient church of St Boniface, just 48 feet long and with space for just eighty worshippers, was not able to seat all those who wished to attend. Its minuscule size mercifully spared it from the restorers: in the late 1840s it was found more convenient to build a new church on ground close by, part-bequeathed by the Swinburne family.

St Boniface was built on an ancient site. The atmosphere is romantic and sublime, bosky and damp, with a stream purling by, and water cascading noisily down to the sea far below. After the old church had been deserted it fell gently into a long sleep. Ivy colonised the porch and roofs and creeper wound its way over the old fabric.

The poet Swinburne was born at East Dene, a long, low house set close by the church. He spent many hours wandering the paths of the old overgrown churchyard and the wooded slopes of the down. Phrases from his evocative poem 'A Forsaken Garden' summon up the deeply romantic atmosphere:

In a coign of the cliff between
lowland and highland,
At the sea-down's edge between
windward and lee, …
If a step should sound or a word
be spoken,
Would a ghost not rise at the strange
guest's hand? …
Through branches and briars if
a man make way,
He shall find no life but the
sea-wind's, restless
Night and day.

Swinburne died in 1909 and his funeral took place in his beloved church. He was buried beside other members of his family among tall grasses in the old overgrown churchyard.

Cases to Delight and Edify

SOME LATE VICTORIAN MUSEUMS AND THEIR EXHIBITS

THE PHOTOGRAPH of the museum at Haslemere (BELOW) shows how we might imagine the classic Victorian museum to have been: row upon row of glass-topped cabinets stuffed with shards of rock and dusty crayfish, and glass domes containing disconsolate-looking stuffed owls and rodents. Everything appears dead and lifeless, shut away from the sunlight. There are few labels for visitors in search of enlightenment. We can still enter small town museums today and experience the same eclectic mixture of exhibits, often with their labels yellowing and curling. We are either attracted or repelled by them.

Compared with today's museums, with their beautifully conceived and constructed displays, sophisticated graphics and temperature-controlled galleries, the Haslemere museum appears distinctly amateurish and uninformative. Yet it was ground-breaking in concept. Its founder, the eminent surgeon Joseph Hutchinson, established it in 1888, with an almost religious zeal for reform and education. His museum 'took its beginning from a wish to try to see how far such collections might be made useful as a means of popular instruction'. He aimed at 'supplying the means of obtaining knowledge to many thousands, who will none of them ever themselves become collectors or attempt any original work'. It was indeed a praiseworthy aim.

Below:
Joseph Hutchinson's Museum at Haslemere, Surrey 1899 44466

Hutchinson moved his museum to spacious new wooden buildings in 1894 (ABOVE). They housed the first temporary displays of living specimens, with up to a hundred examples of mosses in spring, flowers in summer, fungi in winter, and bell glasses and tanks containing swimming newts, fairy shrimps, and water beetles. No attempt was made to exhibit any botanical rarities, only the common objects of the countryside. They proved hugely popular with the groups of school children who visited and filled the chairs that line the sheds.

Yet they were only the overture for Hutchinson's truly visionary view of earth history - his 'Space for Time' method of display. In one of the long sheds, the walls were sub-divided into thirty-five compartments, each division representing a million years of geological time. On shelves in each section were placed specimens or drawings of fossils appropriate to the period. Hutchinson found this to be a simple but effective way of demonstrating the vast duration of earth history, the order and relative length of each period, and the succession of animal and vegetable life. It must be remembered that it was only thirty years since Darwin had published his revolutionary 'Origin of Species', and many devout Churchmen were still uneasy about denying the truth of the Creation story in Genesis.

Joseph Hutchinson died in 1913, but his museum lived on, and moved to its present position in Haslemere High

Street in 1926.

Cheltenham College Museum, established in 1870, was very different from Hutchinson's, being more traditional in function and intent. The building (BELOW) was converted from a racquets court for an outlay of £700, and new cases were constructed at a cost of £50. The College was mindful of its investment in the project, but felt certain that advantages would 'accrue to the College' when the Museum became known and fully appreciated. The first curator was Thomas Bloxham, the Master in Experimental and Natural Sciences.

The Museum aimed at interesting the college's pupils 'in the study of science and natural history', whilst at the same time offering them 'an attractive and useful recreation during their play hours'. (Boys would surely wish for leisure pursuits a little less educational and edifying). A significant collection of fossils and minerals was given by the Cheltenham Naturalists Society, and Mr Charles Pierson, who was at one time Director of the College, donated his 'large and valuable collection of geological specimens'. The museum catalogue offers a flavour of what was on view to pupils in 1870: skins of grass snake, some flint implements, a bandolier, a Mauser carbine, a flag, a Boer hat, three stuffed bears, two stuffed heads of elk, four cases of birds, an elephant's foot, a human skull, a grasshopper in a bottle and some Indian coins. It was clearly a much less focused and more random collection when compared with Hutchinson's. In 1877 the *Cheltenham Examiner* lamented the 'very scanty numbers of persons' visiting the Museum - it was open to the public one

Below:
Cheltenham
College Museum
(later the Pierson
Museum),
Gloucestershire
1907
59043

afternoon each week. Nevertheless, attendance picked up and the Museum grew to be a great success.

In 1883 it was renamed the Pierson Museum in honour of its most generous donor, and was considerably enlarged and expanded over the years. When war broke out in 1939 the museum was packed up and put into store. The collection was finally dispersed in 1976, with many of the exhibits going to the Merseyside Museum.

The photograph of the display of artefacts at Old Sarum in Wiltshire (ABOVE) was doubtless intended for a very different audience. It is possibly a wooden hut on site offering temporary storage for excavated objects. Here archaeologists would come to check the progress of the excavation and to inspect finds made by diggers. The lack of information labels suggests that the display was intended for viewing by professionals only. There is a single sign - 'Please do not touch'. Half-obscured, it is unlikely it would have been obeyed by excited archaeologists.

Old Sarum is the site of an Iron Age fort, a Roman road junction, a Norman castle and a medieval cathedral town, the original city of Salisbury. The artefacts shown are from the excavation of the cathedral and inner bailey carried out between 1909 and 1915 by the Society of Antiquaries under Sir William St John Hope. One notable find was a quantity of very rare pieces of verde-outico and red porphyry. It is likely that the items on the second shelf down show the pieces reconstructed into jugs and pots.

Other items on the shelves include iron keys, some fragments of Norman stonework and animal bones.

For Those in Peril

THE STORY OF THE ALDEBURGH AND CROMER LIFEBOATMEN

THE EAST ANGLIAN coast has always been treacherous to mariners. In 1779 the poet George Crabbe, who was born in the Suffolk town of Aldeburgh, reported on a severe storm that battered the front, writing that 'the breakers dash over the roofs, curl round the walls and crush all to ruins'. Eleven houses were claimed by the sea, and Crabbe's own house was deluged in water four feet deep, forcing the family to retreat to the first floor.

The lot of the fisherman's family could be a tragic one. The East Anglian fishermen ventured out in modest-sized beach yawls open to the waves, and were often obliged to row against rough seas. In his poem 'The Borough' Crabbe tells of the dreadful forebodings of those left on shore:

*'Hark! To those sounds! They're from distress at sea:
How quick they come! What terrors may there be!
Yes, 'tis a driven vessel: I discern
Lights, signs of terror, gleaming from the stern ...
In various parties seamen hurry down;
Their wives pursue, and damsels urged by dread ...'*

In George Crabbe's era there were no lifeboats; the service was only established in 1824. It was not until 1851 that Aldeburgh was given its own lifeboat, and it was kept busy during the months of foul weather, when gales blew for days on end, whipping up violent seas. Barques and brigs were continually driven ashore off Aldeburgh, or forced aground and wrecked on the many sand banks a short distance offshore. The Aldeburgh crew had to put out in all weathers to offer assistance, battling against mountainous surf to row their vessel out into open water. Their courage and persistence saved many lives. Rescue calls were not always brief affairs: in 1881 the Aldeburgh boat stayed at sea in a dreadful snowstorm

for almost thirty hours, having sailed a total of 120 miles.

On 7 December 1899 the lifeboat was called to the aid of a stricken vessel that had run aground on the sands, but was suddenly struck broadside by two huge waves, causing twelve crewmen to be flung overboard. Six lifeboatmen perished, and the whole country was shocked by the disaster. A fund was set up for the dependents.

The Aldeburgh lifeboat 'City of Winchester' is shown in the opening photograph of this chapter. Launched in 1902, she was a Norfolk and Suffolk

type boat, built at Blackwall by the Thames Ironworks boatyard. She cost £2,640, and the money was funded by public subscription in the city of Winchester. Forty-six feet in length, she gives an impression of being sturdy, but was non-self-righting. The crew had to row her through the heavy surf until they could manage to raise the sails, and then still find the strength to carry out the rescue. The 'Winchester' saved many lives, going to the aid of a number of steam ships, yachts and ketches. She was finally taken out of service in 1928.

Aldeburgh's most celebrated lifeboat-man was James Cable, who became coxswain in 1888. He retired in 1917, after fifty years of service, during which he received three Silver Medals from the R.N.L.I. and the Norwegian Silver Medal. He was also presented with a silver cigarette case by a lady after saving her three daughters from drowning.

The picture (LEFT) shows the crew of the Cromer lifeboat 'Louisa Heartwell' in 1922. Like the Aldeburgh men, the fourteen-man crew holding aloft the

Above:
The Esplanade,
Aldeburgh,
Suffolk 1894
33355

oars were volunteers, who in addition to working as builders, shopkeepers, fishermen and the like, were ready to drop what they were doing to exchange leisure, comfort and sleep for cold, wet, fatigue and whatever horrors the North Sea could throw at them. The lifeboat station, with its timbered gable wall, can be seen at the top of the slipway in the photograph of rough seas (BELOW).

Henry Blogg, the most decorated lifeboatman in the long history of the service, is the coxswain of the 'Louisa Heartwell' in the picture (PREVIOUS PAGE). He was in charge of the Cromer boat from 1909 to 1947, earning three gold medals, four silver, the George Cross and the British Empire Medal. During his fifty-three years as a lifeboatman the Cromer boat saved 873 lives.

Other crew members are displaying their medals in the picture: during the War in 1917, William Davie and Stewart Holmes gained silver medals along with Henry Blogg in going to the assistance of the Swedish steamer 'Fernebo', which was blown in half after striking a mine in a terrific gale. The Cromer crew, having only just returned from saving another vessel, turned their boat straight around and without a word of complaint headed straight back into the high seas. They won commendations from other nations, too - Henry Blogg received awards from the Queen of Holland and from the Italian and French governments for saving the lives of their nationals.

Conditions could always turn out to be treacherous; in 1941 Blogg was washed out of the lifeboat with five of his crew while rescuing the crew of the 'English Trader' - he was sixty-five, an age when most of us are feeling it is time we put our feet up for a well-earned rest.

Below:
The Lifeboat Station, Cromer, Norfolk 1902
49059

Opposite:
Lifeboatmen 1906
56543

In Search of the Silver Darlings

THE FISHERMEN OF THE NORTH-EAST COASTS OF BRITAIN

HUNTING the herring was a perilous business, but when the drift nets were hauled and were near bursting with fish, it was a time for rejoicing. The Scottish poet Hugh Macdiarmid, born in 1892, expresses the fisherman's deep passion for his calling:

> O it's ain o' the bonniest
> sichts in the warld
> To watch the herrin' come
> walkin' on board
> In the wee sma' 'oors o'
> a simmer's mornin'
> As if o' their ain accord.

Chasing the 'silver darlings' (a common name for the herring) began as an industry in Scotland during the 17th century. In 1808, when Fishery Officers first branded barrels of Scotch herring with a crown, the symbol of assured quality, expansion was rapid. A few years later there were also significant improvements in the methods of curing: herring shoals were pursued in deep seas far from the harbour, and the journey home was too long for the fish to be sold and eaten fresh. Some method of preserving them was essential, and the herring were normally salted and dried. Herring were particularly nutritious, and were sought after as a staple part of the Victorian diet.

The number of boats drifting for herring increased, and gutting and curing houses sprang up in the ports of the north-east and Scotland. The combined industry of the region was the greatest in the world.

In Scotland, drifting for herring was particularly hazardous, for the Scots fishers were wedded to their open boats. At Fraserburgh (LEFT), a major port on the north-east coast, the harbour is packed solid with open boats from ports around the region. The scene here is frenzied and boisterous: men are arranging the tackle ready for sailing, and folding and stowing the huge drift nets with their floats. The vessel in the foreground is from Nairn, further west along the Moray Firth. Though she is broad in the beam, her decking is shallow, and would offer scant protection in the violent storms that are common in the North Sea.

In 1848 there was a tragic disaster when a hundred fishermen were lost in a ferocious south-easterly gale. There were many widows and fatherless children. Despite an enquiry and a strong appeal for a change to safer decked luggers, the Scottish fishermen and, surprisingly, their own Fisheries Board, remained unconvinced by the arguments, and

it was not until 1872 that the first decked boat was built.

There would be as much activity on shore as on the boats themselves. The Scottish fishwives and their children were busy knitting jerseys, collecting mussels for bait, and mending nets. Often they had to do the job of selling the fish as well: when landings were late owing to bad weather, they were obliged to haul the laden baskets of fish

several miles to the markets to negotiate with wholesalers.

The industry was strictly seasonal, which led to major migrations of labour from port to port. The fishing harbours were often thronged with men and women working desperately to meet the sailing schedules, ensuring that catches were not forfeited and vital income lost.

Further south at the attractive fishing village of Staithes in Yorkshire, which is tucked between two steep headlands, Whitby-built yawls and cobles ventured out in pairs to take the haddock, cod and mackerel. Each of the yawls had a ten-man crew and the cobles that trailed them three-man crews. When the yawls were sinking under the weight of fish, the catch was transferred to the cobles. There were three hundred vessels at Staithes in the 1850s. The larger vessels followed the shoals, and ventured as far south as Yarmouth each September to join the huge East Anglian herring fleets.

The photograph of Staithes in 1890 (OPPOSITE) shows fish wives and old men baiting the lines. It was an interminable and thankless task. A contemporary writer describes the atmosphere: 'On the shore were bare-legged urchins and dead herrings - with the natural result of a fishy odour. Yet for all that there is an air of prosperity about the place'. Visitors were drawn to watch the scene: 'few will regret delaying their steps awhile to visit this Elysium of primitive simplicity'. It was hardly Elysium for the fishermen and their families, but it was certainly picturesque to the casual observer. The women wore traditional bonnets which were flared at the sides to stop the coils of hooks and line becoming entangled in their hair. Each bonnet required a yard of material, and

was double-plaited at the front and tied at the back with a bow.

At the Grimsby fish pontoon (ABOVE) the daily auction is under way, and the crates are overflowing with fish that will soon be on their way to London.

Here, the fishing industry was much stimulated by the building of the Manchester, Sheffield and Lincolnshire railway in 1852, which opened up vital new inland markets. Trawlers and smacks laboured to feed the hungry mouths of Britain, landing catches of sole, haddock, plaice, turbot, halibut, cod and whiting. By the time of the photograph their numbers had been augmented by bigger and more powerful steam trawlers.

However, the boom was past. The steam vessels had been too effective at their work. Over-fishing had caused an inevitable drop in catches, and the east coast and Scottish ports suffered an irreversible decline. The numbers of commercial boats at the quays diminished. It was the end of a way of life.

Above:
The Fish
Pontoon,
Grimsby,
Lincolnshire 1906
55748

Scratting for the Poor Man's Oyster

GATHERING THE RICHES OF THE SANDS AND SHORES AROUND BRITAIN

THE SANDS and shores at low tide have riches for the hungry. For fishermen and those that live by the sea, there are cockles to rake out of the sand, winkles to pick out of rock pools, shrimps to net, limpets to prise from rocks, and clams to dig.

The old Llanmadog woman (OPPOSITE) is 'scratting' (scratching) the sands of the Welsh Gower Peninsula for the dark-coloured Devon cockles. She is watching for the tell-tale pair of small holes which betray the cockle's presence an inch or so below the surface. Her cuffs are cut away to prevent them from drawing cold seawater up her arms, her skirt is tucked up, and her scarf tied tight as a bandage around her hat. With her stockings cut away at the ankles, she paddles barefoot in the freezing water, bent double for hours on end over the cold sands. Back in the village, she will sell some to the fishmonger then steam a few others in a saucepan for her dinner.

The writer Ernest Pulbrook chose several Frith pictures, including this one, for his famous survey 'English Country Life and Work', published in 1922. 'Quaint are the women cockle gatherers', he says. They may well have looked quaint to him from the comfort of his hotel window. Whilst he was enjoying his afternoon tea this old woman was trudging across the flats against a headwind, hauling a basket that got ever heavier. But we can perhaps forgive him: he wrote his book as a passionate testament to a vanishing age

and to generations of country people, including hardy fishing communities, who battled with the sea to make ends meet.

The cockle shells that are found on the surface are always empty. You will find live cockles just inches down in the sand. Often you will see a siphon of water where a cockle is drawing down air. You should only gather the cockles that you cannot prise open with your fingers. Never toss them into the basket, for you may break the shells. And if you gather them today, make sure you are not close to a sewage outfall.

The cockle-men of the North Norfolk coast (BELOW) turned a pastime into an industry. They have been out in their boats, 'Nell' and 'Armistice', across the

Opposite:
Old Cockle Woman, Llanmadog, West Glamorgan 1906
53961

Below:
Bringing in the Cockles, Wells-next-the-Sea, Norfolk 1929
82003

Below:
Collecting
Seaweed, Inverary,
Argyll c1890
I15002

Bottom:
Fishwives, Tenby,
Pembrokeshire
1890
28091

flat salt marshes, and have returned with a considerable haul in their nets. They use yokes to ease the burden.

The South Wales fishwives (BOTTOM) have been shrimping with nets on the sands and filling the baskets they carry on their backs. The old walled town of Tenby was a highly popular watering-place in the far south-west of Wales, and these women have been paddling in the shallows on South Beach facing the broad seaward sweep that takes in Caldy Island and the Gower Peninsula. They will hawk their catch on the beach and quayside. They are wearing traditional Welsh shawls draped around their shoulders and long heavy skirts.

After storms, beaches on some parts of Britain's coasts can be strewn to a depth of several feet with seaweed. At St Michael's Mount in south Cornwall, the farmers were down on the beach with their cart by two o'clock in the morning, as soon as the winds and seas had abated. They collected the seaweed which they used as a free fertilizer for their sour land.

At Inverary (LEFT), on the shores of Loch Fyne, men and women are heaping the scattered weed into baskets. Others form the mass into a ball, tie it with string and then haul it away on their backs. It is not comfortable work, for the sands are slippery and the weed slithers through chilled fingers. Some seaweeds are edible, especially the excellent lava weed, with its translucent purple fronds.

Sun, Thrills and Spills

THE RISE OF THE GREAT BRITISH HOLIDAY

QUEEN VICTORIA was one of the first women to venture into a bathing machine, dipping herself gingerly into the waters of the Channel in 1847. Closely attended by a 'very nice bathing woman' she relished the experience. On Blackpool's North Beach (BELOW), rival firms are competing for trade. Penswick, Singleton and Smith machines are drawn up on the sands. They are smothered in advertisements for Sunlight Soap and Jones' Sewing

Left:
Paddling at
Weymouth,
Dorset 1909
61597

Below:
Bathing Machines
at Blackpool,
Lancashire 1890
22886

Machines. Mr Singleton has converted the top machine into an office. Ladies would undress in the privacy of the machines, which were hauled by horses down the beach and into the water on chains. Protected and chaperoned, these intrepid bathers stepped discreetly down into the shallows unseen.

Right:
Flying Machine, Blackpool, Lancashire 1906
53857

Below:
Donkeys at Rhyl, Clywd 1891
29151

The diarist the Rev. Francis Kilvert detested the custom of bathing in drawers. 'If ladies don't like to see men naked why don't they keep out of sight?' One day in 1874 on the Isle of Wight, rough waves stripped off his drawers and tore them down round his ankles. He was seized and flung down by a heavy sea and left stranded on the shingle. 'After this I took the wretched rag off and of course there were ladies looking on as I came up out of the water.'

Blackpool formed an irresistible attraction for the millions of ordinary working people who toiled for long hours in the mills and factories of the industrial north. They looked forward eagerly to their days out away from the grime and noise of the factory floor, and for the chance to display their best hats

Left:
**Dancing on the
Beach, Newquay,
Cornwall 1912**
64790a

Below:
**Black and White
Minstrels,
Lytham,
Lancashire 1914**
67479

and new parasols. The town was renowned for its wonders of architecture and engineering: apart from three piers, the famous Tower opened in 1894 and a big wheel in 1896. A queue of excited trippers waits to experience the thrills of the flying boats (OPPOSITE, TOP). It is impossible for us to imagine the sheer unbridled excitement of a ride on these massive flying boats, which flung the riders far out into the sky and whirled them round at breathtaking speed, for in their everyday lives most Victorians rarely travelled much above walking pace. The experience must have been unforgettable.

Down on the beach there was always just as much to enjoy. There were rides along the sands on donkeys at Rhyl in North Wales (OPPOSITE, LEFT), and black and white minstrels to entertain the crowds at Lytham just down the coast from Blackpool (RIGHT). At Newquay in Cornwall (TOP) bandsmen assembled to play the tunes of the day, and holiday-makers danced in rings.

Left:
The Pier,
Eastbourne,
Sussex 1925
77946

Seaside piers began life as landing stages for steamers offering trips round the bay. Soon they became popular places to promenade, where holiday-makers could savour the bracing sea air and look back to enjoy exhilarating prospects of the coast and townscape. Piers were masterful feats of engineering, elegant and exotic, thrusting far out into the sea with characteristic Victorian aplomb. The Victorian entrepreneur was never slow in recognising commercial potential: modest piers were enlarged to make space for seats, kiosks, bandstands and pavilions. They became fashionable places to see and be seen. By the early 1900s they were the focus for seaside fun, and thousands pushed through the turnstiles to enter a world far removed from their workaday lives.

In the photograph of Eastbourne on the south coast (LEFT), charabancs are touting for business at the pier. The nearest is bound for Pevensey Bay, where the passengers will marvel at the Martello towers, circle the battlements at the castle, and then retire to the tearoom for some welcome refreshment. Meanwhile, passengers in the other charabanc will be enjoying the fresh air of the South Downs. Those with strong stomachs will peer dizzily down from Beachy Head at the matchstick-sized lighthouse hundreds of feet below. Then, holding hats firmly down with two hands, they will be up and over the downs, heading back to Eastbourne.

The Victorians invented the seaside. Many of the attractions that they enjoyed are still being enjoyed today - the piers, promenades, fairground rides, and trips round the bay. We have them to thank for the Great British Holiday that so many of us continue to look forward to today.

Tea and Chaucer on Colley Hill

THE PUBLIC CELEBRATION AT THE ACQUISITION OF COLLEY HILL NEAR REIGATE BY THE NATIONAL TRUST

'KNIGHT *and yeoman, squire and lawyer, miller, monk and nun ... a motley crew, with bells and bagpipes, minstrels and buffoons, all making their way with infinite clatter and jest, and talking incessantly in many tongues ...'*

This is not Chaucer writing in the 14th century *Canterbury Times*, but H. J. Foley, a reporter for the *Surrey Mirror*, on the Canterbury Pilgrims' Pageant at Colley Hill, Reigate, in 1913.

On a sweltering June day, many thousands celebrated the acquisition of sixty acres of this beautiful chalk upland by the National Trust, who after an arduous fund-raising campaign had bought the land for the people for £5000. Over this down, along the ancient track, the Pilgrims' Way, pilgrims had travelled over the centuries to the grave of St Thomas à Becket at Canterbury.

Sir Robert Hunter, Chairman of the National Trust, addressing the assembled crowd, was relieved that in a time when 'people were fond of living in high places', that this potentially 'magnificent building land' had been saved and 'a calamity averted'. He went on to say that the highlands of the Home Counties were the natural playground for the enormous population of London - a population then larger than the whole of Scotland and the whole of Australia. Sir Robert, looking ahead, speculated whether Colley Hill would in future times end up as a green oasis in the midst of an enormously enlarged metropolis. To avert this possible tragedy, he believed it was vital that every open space within fifty miles of London should be secured for public amenity and not squandered for building land.

His vision has been in no small measure vindicated: though houses have spread in a rash over the hills of the North Downs, there is still a very special atmosphere of space and quietness there.

Lord Curzon, resplendent in top hat, presided over the ceremony. He had lived a few miles further along the track near Box Hill, and knew 'every yard of the hill with its beautiful woodland, and its intervening verge, almost like bouquets of box and juniper and thorn'. Can we imagine a public figure speaking so poetically now? A ceremony always brought out the romantic in a true Englishman at the beginning of the 20th century.

Lord Curzon spoke feelingly about the importance of saving this 'portion of the national heritage of England'. *The Surrey Mirror and County Post* reported his impassioned rhetoric:

Colley Hill would be an outlet for the population, stunned by the noise, fatigued by the burden of life in London. Some of them who lived in the city felt as if their spirit were crushed by vanloads of brick and mortar. In some parts of the year they were stifled by the smoke, in others choked by the fog; London was like a great octopus stretching out to lay hold on the leafy lanes of the countryside. They had to defeat it. (Cheers)

The pageant, though considerably under-rehearsed, was a triumph of local effort, with five hundred costumed figures forming a 'seemingly never-ending

Lord Curzon
Addressing the
Crowds at Colley
Hill, Reigate,
Surrey 1913
R20304 (right)
R20308 (below)

procession' across the face of the down. Everyone was there - including Robin Hood, Maid Marion and Henry VIII. The *Surrey Mirror* reported that there were sixteen groups of pilgrims, each under a leader, who entered the ring of the local horse-show ground where a march-past took place. Judges selected four groups, which they judged to be of equal merit from the historical and artistic point of view.

The final winner was the group under Mr Tatton Winter, which dealt with the period 1400-1450: it represented a lady and gentleman of the time and his suite, with his daughter riding, attended by a page; an abbess followed, over whom was held a canopy, and who was carrying a sacred relic to the holy shrine at Canterbury. Behind were the retainers and servants, with the serjeant at law.

Similar national appeals to save monuments of national importance are made by the National Trust today: our landscape and architectural heritage are still under threat, and an appeal made through the colour and atmosphere of British history remains a potent weapon in the fight to gather sufficient funding.

Above:
Historical Figures from the Colley Hill Pageant 1913
R20310a

Left:
The March Past, Colley Hill Pageant 1913
R20310b

Pandemonium on the Water

JEROME K JEROME'S QUEST FOR THE QUIET LIFE ON THE RIVER THAMES

Below:
**Coming Over
the Rollers,
River Thames,
East Molesey 1896**
38346

RIVER OUTINGS on the Thames were so popular that in 1889 Jerome K Jerome embarked on the tale of one of the most famous boat trips in the history of English literature. His book 'Three Men in a Boat' recounts a quest for peace and quiet on the Thames, and sold an astonishing two million copies in his lifetime.

Jerome's narrator felt that he and his colleagues were 'overworked and in need of a rest'. Where better to go than the Thames, with its spacious reaches and tranquil backwaters? They found that they had seriously miscalculated. Jerome tells of the bedlam at Molesey Lock, where 'you could not see any

water at all, but only a brilliant tangle of bright blazers, and gay caps, and saucy hats, and many-coloured parasols, and silken rugs, and cloaks, and streaming ribbons, and dainty whites'.

In the Frith photograph (BELOW) it looks plain pandemonium, with punts and skiffs forcing their passage in every direction. Another Victorian writer, Richard Jefferies, in his essay 'The Modern Thames', pointed out that to survive you had to pull and push and struggle for your existence on the river, convinced that yours is the very best style of rowing, and that everyone else

should get out of your way. If you were in any doubt about your rights, the only course of action was drive hard into other people's boats, forcing them into the bank. Most important of all, you should never look ahead, but pull straight on. It was a capital sport, too, to splash the ladies with a dextrous flip of the scull and do your best to soak their summer costumes.

Jerome's narrator did not take to the town of Maidenhead. It is the haunt of the 'river swell and his overdressed female companion', he said. 'It is the town of showy hotels, patronised chiefly by dudes and ballet girls. It is the witch's kitchen from which go forth those demons of the river - steam launches'. At the busy Boulter's Lock, Maidenhead (ABOVE), steam launches are hogging the water. Smaller punts and skiffs are obliged to hang impotently about their skirts.

Steam launches carrying trippers never gave way to small boats like Jerome's, and ruined the easy life of the river. The narrator admits to a deep loathing of steam launches, for there was a 'blatant bumptiousness' about them. The boat trip Jerome describes

Above:
Entrance to Boulters Lock, Maidenhead, River Thames 1906
54083

was continually punctuated by lordly whistles from the decks of steam launches demanding that they get out of the way. Jerome's narrator nursed a deep desire to 'lure one to a lonely part of the river, and there, in the silence and the solitude, strangle it.'

Some Thames sailors found contentment, however. No one can look as lazy as the Victorians at leisure. The picture (BELOW) shows a party on a steam launch at Molesey Lock on the Thames in 1896. Luncheon has been consumed, the hampers are empty, and only the wrapping remains. The two housemaids enjoy a few moments' well-earned rest, and they will need it - they have been hard at work since dawn. A Victorian picnic meant more than a plate of cucumber sandwiches. Mrs Beeton decreed that no self-respecting picnicker should venture out without a hamper overflowing with joints of cold roast beef, fowls, parcels of duck, ham, tongue, veal pie, pigeon pie, lobster, and a collared calf's head, to be followed by stewed fruit, cabinet pudding, jam puffs and plum cake; all of the foregoing to be washed down with sherry, claret, ginger beer and champagne. No wonder the ladies have stretched themselves out.

If he failed to discover peace himself, Jerome's narrator denied others theirs. At one stage, near Cookham, he spotted a fishing-punt on which were three 'old and solemn-looking men'. They were sitting on chairs watching their lines intently. 'And the red sunset threw a mystic light upon the waters ... and it was an hour of deep enchantment.' Jerome's narrator was steering when, for a few unfortunate moments, his sail put the punt out of view. The next he knew they had gone slap bang into it.

Below:
Houseboats in Lock,
East Molesey,
River Thames
1896
38350

He and his fellow crew were cursed for their carelessness, 'not with a common cursory curse, but with long, carefully thought-out, comprehensive curses, that embraced the whole of our career … and included all our relations.'

The view of children fishing at Bray (RIGHT) suggests that it was safer to fish from dry land. These children are enjoying angling in the shallows while their parents are lunching in the George Hotel behind.

Jerome says that at Streatley (ABOVE) 'The Angler's Guide to the Thames' reports that 'jack and perch are to be had about here'. Jerome's narrator saw them, for they came out of the water to

him with their mouths open for biscuits, and crowded round and got in his way whenever he went over the side for a bathe. 'But they were not to be had by a bit of a worm on the end of a hook, nor anything like it - not they'.

Above:
The Swan Hotel, Streatley, River Thames 1899
42994

Left:
Children Fishing at Bray, River Thames 1890
23621

Index of Places

Acknowledgements

I should like to thank the following for their help in providing information about the photographs in this book:

Catherine Baird, North Shropshire District Council

Barry Baldwin, Corsham

Calderdale Council Leisure Services

Mr Callund, Cookham

Geoff Chapman, Chillington

Nina Curtis, Clovelly Post Office

English Heritage

Richard Grasby, Bedchester

Haslemere Educational Museum

Miss Hebden, Malvern Museum

Peter Hill, Pell Wall

The Honiton Lace Shop

Alun Jenkins, Ewenny Pottery

Mrs Christine Leighton, Cheltenham College

Lord Louis Library, Newport, Isle of Wight

Maidenhead Reference Library

Mr Michael Marshman, Wiltshire County Local Studies Librarian

Mrs Dorothy Merrin, Knaresborough

Mr P A Owen, Hindhead Golf Club

Mrs Perryman, Allhallows Lace Museum, Honiton

Pickles of Knaresborough

Mr D S G Reid, Royal National Lifeboat Institution, Aldeburgh

Mrs Patricia Saunders, King Edward VII Hospital, Midhurst

Surrey Local Studies Library

John Symonds, Chillington

Uttlesford District Council

Mr D H Williams, Criccieth Golf Club

Frith Book Co Titles

www.francisfrith.co.uk

The Frith Book Company publishes over 100 new titles each year. A selection of those currently available are listed below. For latest catalogue please contact Frith Book Co.

Town Books 96pages, approx 100 photos. County and Themed Books 128pages, approx 150 photos (unless specified). All titles hardback laminated case and jacket except those indicated pb (paperback)

Ancient Monuments & Stone Circles		
	1-85937-143-4	£17.99
Aylesbury (pb)	1-85937-227-9	£9.99
Bakewell	1-85937-113-2	£12.99
Barnstaple (pb)	1-85937-300-3	£9.99
Bath	1-85937-097-7	£12.99
Bedford (pb)	1-85937-205-8	£9.99
Berkshire (pb)	1-85937-191-4	£9.99
Berkshire Churches	1-85937-170-1	£17.99
Bognor Regis (pb)	1-85937-431-x	£9.99
Bournemouth	1-85937-067-5	£12.99
Bradford (pb)	1-85937-204-x	£9.99
Brighton & Hove (pb)	1-85937-192-2	£8.99
Bristol (pb)	1-85937-264-3	£9.99
British Life A Century Ago (pb)	1-85937-213-9	£9.99
Buckinghamshire (pb)	1-85937-200-7	£9.99
Camberley (pb)	1-85937-222-8	£9.99
Cambridge (pb)	1-85937-422-0	£9.99
Cambridgeshire (pb)	1-85937-420-4	£9.99
Canals & Waterways (pb)	1-85937-291-0	£9.99
Canterbury Cathedral (pb)	1-85937-179-5	£9.99
Cardiff (pb)	1-85937-093-4	£9.99
Carmarthenshire	1-85937-216-3	£14.99
Cheltenham (pb)	1-85937-095-0	£9.99
Cheshire (pb)	1-85937-271-6	£9.99
Chester	1-85937-090-x	£12.99
Chesterfield	1-85937-071-3	£9.99
Chichester (pb)	1-85937-228-7	£9.99
Colchester (pb)	1-85937-188-4	£8.99
Cornish Coast	1-85937-163-9	£14.99
Cornwall (pb)	1-85937-229-5	£9.99
Cornwall Living Memories	1-85937-248-1	£14.99
Cotswolds (pb)	1-85937-230-9	£9.99
Cotswolds Living Memories	1-85937-255-4	£14.99
County Durham	1-85937-123-x	£14.99
Cumbria	1-85937-101-9	£14.99
Dartmoor	1-85937-145-0	£14.99
Derbyshire (pb)	1-85937-196-5	£9.99
Devon (pb)	1-85937-297-x	£9.99
Dorset (pb)	1-85937-269-4	£9.99
Dorset Churches	1-85937-172-8	£17.99
Dorset Coast (pb)	1-85937-299-6	£9.99

Dorset Living Memories	1-85937-210-4	£14.99
Down the Severn	1-85937-118-3	£14.99
Down the Thames (pb)	1-85937-278-3	£9.99
Dublin (pb)	1-85937-231-7	£9.99
East Anglia (pb)	1-85937-265-1	£9.99
East London	1-85937-080-2	£14.99
East Sussex	1-85937-130-2	£14.99
Eastbourne	1-85937-061-6	£12.99
Edinburgh (pb)	1-85937-193-0	£8.99
English Castles (pb)	1-85937-434-4	£9.99
English Country Houses	1-85937-161-2	£17.99
Exeter	1-85937-126-4	£12.99
Exmoor	1-85937-132-9	£14.99
Falmouth	1-85937-066-7	£12.99
Folkestone (pb)	1-85937-124-8	£9.99
Glasgow (pb)	1-85937-190-6	£9.99
Gloucestershire	1-85937-102-7	£14.99
Greater Manchester (pb)	1-85937-266-x	£9.99
Hampshire Churches (pb)	1-85937-207-4	£9.99
Harrogate	1-85937-423-9	£9.99
Hastings & Bexhill (pb)	1-85937-131-0	£9.99
Heart of Lancashire (pb)	1-85937-197-3	£9.99
Helston (pb)	1-85937-214-7	£9.99
Hereford (pb)	1-85937-175-2	£9.99
Herefordshire	1-85937-174-4	£14.99
Humberside	1-85937-215-5	£14.99
Hythe, Romney Marsh & Ashford	1-85937-256-2	£9.99
Ipswich (pb)	1-85937-424-7	£9.99
Ireland (pb)	1-85937-181-7	£9.99
Isles of Scilly	1-85937-136-1	£14.99
Isle of Wight (pb)	1-85937-429-8	£9.99
Isle of Wight Living Memories	1-85937-304-6	£14.99
Kent (pb)	1-85937-189-2	£9.99
Kent Living Memories	1-85937-125-6	£14.99
Lake District (pb)	1-85937-275-9	£9.99
Lancaster, Morecambe & Heysham (pb)		
	1-85937-233-3	£9.99
Leeds (pb)	1-85937-202-3	£9.99
Leicester	1-85937-073-x	£12.99
Leicestershire (pb)	1-85937-185-x	£9.99
Lighthouses	1-85937-257-0	£17.99
Lincolnshire (pb)	1-85937-433-6	£9.99

Available from your local bookshop or from the publisher

Frith Book Co Titles (continued)

Title	ISBN	Price	Title	ISBN	Price
Liverpool & Merseyside (pb)	1-85937-234-1	£9.99	Southampton (pb)	1-85937-427-1	£9.99
London (pb)	1-85937-183-3	£9.99	Southport (pb)	1-85937-425-5	£9.99
Ludlow (pb)	1-85937-176-0	£9.99	Stratford upon Avon	1-85937-098-5	£12.99
Luton (pb)	1-85937-235-x	£9.99	Suffolk (pb)	1-85937-221-x	£9.99
Manchester (pb)	1-85937-198-1	£9.99	Suffolk Coast	1-85937-259-7	£14.99
New Forest	1-85937-128-0	£14.99	Surrey (pb)	1-85937-240-6	£9.99
Newport, Wales (pb)	1-85937-258-9	£9.99	Sussex (pb)	1-85937-184-1	£9.99
Newquay (pb)	1-85937-421-2	£9.99	Swansea (pb)	1-85937-167-1	£9.99
Norfolk (pb)	1-85937-195-7	£9.99	Tees Valley & Cleveland	1-85937-211-2	£14.99
Norfolk Living Memories	1-85937-217-1	£14.99	Thanet (pb)	1-85937-116-7	£9.99
Northamptonshire	1-85937-150-7	£14.99	Tiverton (pb)	1-85937-178-7	£9.99
Northumberland Tyne & Wear (pb)	1-85937-281-3	£9.99	Torbay	1-85937-063-2	£12.99
North Devon Coast	1-85937-146-9	£14.99	Truro	1-85937-147-7	£12.99
North Devon Living Memories	1-85937-261-9	£14.99	Victorian and Edwardian Cornwall	1-85937-252-x	£14.99
North Wales (pb)	1-85937-298-8	£9.99	Victorian & Edwardian Devon	1-85937-253-8	£14.99
North Yorkshire (pb)	1-85937-236-8	£9.99	Victorian & Edwardian Kent	1-85937-149-3	£14.99
Norwich (pb)	1-85937-194-9	£8.99	Vic & Ed Maritime Album	1-85937-144-2	£17.99
Nottingham (pb)	1-85937-324-0	£9.99	Victorian and Edwardian Sussex	1-85937-157-4	£14.99
Nottinghamshire (pb)	1-85937-187-6	£9.99	Victorian & Edwardian Yorkshire	1-85937-154-x	£14.99
Peak District (pb)	1-85937-280-5	£9.99	Victorian Seaside	1-85937-159-0	£17.99
Penzance	1-85937-069-1	£12.99	Villages of Devon (pb)	1-85937-293-7	£9.99
Peterborough (pb)	1-85937-219-8	£9.99	Villages of Kent (pb)	1-85937-294-5	£9.99
Piers	1-85937-237-6	£17.99	Warwickshire (pb)	1-85937-203-1	£9.99
Plymouth	1-85937-119-1	£12.99	Welsh Castles (pb)	1-85937-322-4	£9.99
Poole & Sandbanks (pb)	1-85937-251-1	£9.99	West Midlands (pb)	1-85937-289-9	£9.99
Preston (pb)	1-85937-212-0	£9.99	West Sussex	1-85937-148-5	£14.99
Reading (pb)	1-85937-238-4	£9.99	West Yorkshire (pb)	1-85937-201-5	£9.99
Salisbury (pb)	1-85937-239-2	£9.99	Weymouth (pb)	1-85937-209-0	£9.99
St Ives	1-85937-068-3	£12.99	Wiltshire (pb)	1-85937-277-5	£9.99
Scotland (pb)	1-85937-182-5	£9.99	Wiltshire Churches (pb)	1-85937-171-x	£9.99
Scottish Castles (pb)	1-85937-323-2	£9.99	Wiltshire Living Memories	1-85937-245-7	£14.99
Sheffield, South Yorks (pb)	1-85937-267-8	£9.99	Winchester (pb)	1-85937-428-x	£9.99
Shrewsbury (pb)	1-85937-325-9	£9.99	Windmills & Watermills	1-85937-242-2	£17.99
Shropshire (pb)	1-85937-326-7	£9.99	Worcestershire	1-85937-152-3	£14.99
Somerset	1-85937-153-1	£14.99	York (pb)	1-85937-199-x	£9.99
South Devon Coast	1-85937-107-8	£14.99	Yorkshire (pb)	1-85937-186-8	£9.99
South Devon Living Memories	1-85937-168-x	£14.99	Yorkshire Living Memories	1-85937-166-3	£14.99
South Hams	1-85937-220-1	£14.99			

Frith Book Co titles available soon

Title		ISBN	Price	Title		ISBN	Price
1870's England	Oct 01	1-85937-331-3	£17.99	Gloucester (pb)	Oct 01	1-85937-417-4	£9.99
Amersham & Chesham (pb)	Oct 01	1-85937-340-2	£9.99	Oxfordshire (pb)	Oct 01	1-85937-430-1	£9.99
Bedfordshire	Oct 01	1-85937-320-8	£14.99	Picturesque Harbours	Oct 01	1-85937-208-2	£17.99
Belfast (pb)	Oct 01	1-85937-303-8	£9.99	Romford (pb)	Oct 01	1-85937-319-4	£9.99
Britain Living Memories	Oct 01	1-85937-343-7	£17.99	Villages of Sussex (pb)	Sep 01	1-85937-295-3	£9.99
Chelmsford (pb)	Oct 01	1-85937-310-0	£9.99	Worcester (pb)	Oct 01	1-85937-165-5	£9.99

See Frith books on the internet www.francisfrith.co.uk

FRITH PRODUCTS & SERVICES

Francis Frith would doubtless be pleased to know that the pioneering publishing venture he started in 1860 still continues today. A hundred and forty years later, The Francis Frith Collection continues in the same innovative tradition and is now one of the foremost publishers of vintage photographs in the world. Some of the current activities include:

Interior Decoration

Today Frith's photographs can be seen framed and as giant wall murals in thousands of pubs, restaurants, hotels, banks, retail stores and other public buildings throughout the country. In every case they enhance the unique local atmosphere of the places they depict and provide reminders of gentler days in an increasingly busy and frenetic world.

Product Promotions

Frith products are used by many major companies to promote the sales of their own products or to reinforce their own history and heritage. Frith promotions have been used by Hovis bread, Courage beers, Scots Porage Oats, Colman's mustard, Cadbury's foods, Mellow Birds coffee, Dunhill pipe tobacco, Guinness, and Bulmer's Cider.

Genealogy and Family History

As the interest in family history and roots grows world-wide, more and more people are turning to Frith's photographs of Great Britain for images of the towns, villages and streets where their ancestors lived; and, of course, photographs of the churches and chapels where their ancestors were christened, married and buried are an essential part of every genealogy tree and family album.

Frith Products

All Frith photographs are available Framed or just as Mounted Prints and Posters (size 23 x 16 inches). These may be ordered from the address below. From time to time other products - Address Books, Calendars, Table Mats, etc - are available.

The Internet

Already twenty thousand Frith photographs can be viewed and purchased on the internet through the Frith websites and a myriad of partner sites.

For more detailed information on Frith companies and products, look at these sites:

www.francisfrith.co.uk
www.francisfrith.com
(for North American visitors)

See the complete list of Frith Books at:

www.francisfrith.co.uk

This web site is regularly updated with the latest list of publications from the Frith Book Company. If you wish to buy books relating to another part of the country that your local bookshop does not stock, you may purchase on-line.

For further information, trade, or author enquiries please contact us at the address below:
The Francis Frith Collection, Frith's Barn, Teffont, Salisbury, Wiltshire, England SP3 5QP.
Tel: +44 (0)1722 716 376 Fax: +44 (0)1722 716 881 Email: sales@francisfrith.co.uk

See Frith books on the internet www.francisfrith.co.uk